WITNESSING TO DRACULA

A MEMOIR OF MINISTRY IN ROMANIA

by

DR. BILLY NG

Additional copies of this book can be obtained through the author's website at *www.witnessingtodracula.com* or at *www.amazon.com*

Library of Congress Catalog No: 2010901097

ISBN 978-0-615-34943-5

Printed in the United States of America

ACKNOWLEDGEMENTS/DEDICATION

To my Lord and Savior, Jesus Christ.

To my wife, Laura Ng, who endured many single nights while I wrote this book.

To my wonderful readers who labored through my many drafts: Jessica Wyman; Marcella Hopkins; Delores Torres; Allison Sadrianna; Mary Lessner; Diane and John Roberts; Jonathan Forster; Pastor Frank Vernol: Jodi Vernol; Robin Stanziola; and Maryann Bovee - many, many thanks for your kind and honest input. Special thanks goes to Pastor Tony Diuglio for his constructive line-by-line comments.

To the President of ELIM Bible Institute, Jeff Clark, who loves to evangelize the world.

To all the pastors from California to Arizona and to New York who helped in my spiritual growth.

To all the pastors and congregation in Singapore and Malaysia who introduced me to Christ.

To all my colleagues, friends, and family around the globe.

To all the wonderful Romanians whom I met along this incredible journey.

FOREWORD BY JEFF CLARK
PRESIDENT, ELIM BIBLE INSTITUTE, NEW YORK

Witnessing to Dracula is a series of riveting, moving and captivating stories of one of the most exciting church-plants of our day. Cast in the ancient culture of Romania, against the hills of Transylvania, the home of the legend of Count Dracula, Billy Ng takes you on the ride of a lifetime as he goes nose to nose with an ancient culture and religious tradition determined to hedge out the gospel of Jesus Christ.

Born in Malaysia, raised and educated in the U.S., this former Operations professor could not resist the tug of God upon his life to plant a church in the homeland of Count Dracula. A stranger in a strange land, Billy determined that God's grace and love were more powerful weapons than legend and spiritual darkness, opposing the light of God's unconditional love to all of mankind.

I encourage you to set aside some time to journey with my dear friend, Billy Ng, as he extends God's kingdom in the land of Dracula!

CONTENTS

1. Break-Into Ministry

I was always a law abiding person until the day God called me into ministry.

"Give me the hacksaw," I grunted.

"Which do you want?" Credinescu replied, displaying four vicious looking hacksaws.

I looked over the bunch and selected the biggest, meanest one. It was a black carbon model with stainless shark-like teeth. I gripped it with my hand. It felt good, heavy and vicious! It would get the job done. Breaking into a building would be easy with this bad boy. I started sawing at the hardened padlock.

After a few minutes, I was puffing and sweating in the bitter minus twenty degree temperature. Drops of sweat crystallized behind my neck.

"I keep hitting the door," I wheezed to a wide-eyed Credinescu. "I cannot get enough room to push the saw through completely. This big one is of no use! Give me the small orange one. I might have more saw-room then."

Credinescu handed me the small orange saw. I could see that his hands were shaking – more from nervousness than the cold. It was his first time breaking into a building. It was my first time too.

"Don't worry," I said comfortingly. "We will get in. I just need a little bit more time."

Credinescu, Bible in one hand and hacksaws in the other, looked the very picture of misery. The picture of his pastor sawing at a padlock and breaking into a building did not sit well with him.

I started sawing vigorously anew. The little orange saw had razor sharp incisors. As I sawed, my hopes of opening the lock rose only to be squashed just as fast as they had risen. I moaned and groaned and made other disparaging noises.

"I cannot get completely around the lock," I lamented, putting down the saw. "Look! The lock is surrounded by a round solid iron shroud! At this rate, we could be here until next Christmas!"

Credinescu's misery took on a new dimension as he digested this news. He did not want to be around until next Christmas. He grabbed the lock and examined it. He saw the small scratches I had made on it. He let it go with disgust.

At about that time, to compound our nefarious activity, it started to rain ice. I grabbed the metal shroud, with the lock nestling deep inside, and began to study it, hoping to find a weak spot. After a full minute, I came to the conclusion that even Husqvarna's biggest and most powerful chain saw could not make a dent through the super hardened steel. An axe was out of the question too. Too much noise, I thought morbidly. It would have to take a Paul and Silas type miracle to get through all this metal. Furthermore, I was beginning to slide wildly on the thick coat of ice that had formed around the door I was trying to break through.

The day had started off exceptionally well. It was Christmas Eve. Bitingly cold but no snow was forecasted. I liked the 'no-snow' forecast for heavy snow has a way of making people stay at home and away from church.

It was to be my first Christmas Eve program in Romania and I wanted everything to go perfectly. I had planned this event for months. I had downloaded Christmas carols from the internet; the verses had been translated into Romanian; the Praise and Worship team had learned and rehearsed the songs from scratch (after all, none of them had heard of 'Silent Night' and any other type of Christmas carols until now). The song lyrics were now on slides and each slide was made festive with bright holiday colors and other decorations. I had made enough flyers announcing this Christmas Eve program to literally cover a huge chunk of Romania. The flyers had been distributed throughout the community. I had even bought food and drinks for the event. These were stored in the trunk of my car. I made sure I had gas in the tank and I rechecked the car battery several times. In those days, gas stations frequently ran dry and closed for long periods of time.

I was very familiar with the American candlelight Christmas Eve program. It was warm, friendly, and always coupled with great carols. Just before midnight, candles would be lit and 'Silent Night' sung - enough to bring tears to the hardest of hearts.

To mimic such fond sentiments of my life back in the States, I had gone to a local hardware store to purchase some white candles. The store had run out of white. So, I settled for some thin yellow ones instead. I purchased fifty sticks and several boxes of matches.

No project engineer with a detailed computer simulation program could have planned it better. Engineers use simulation programs to build bridges. I was using it to plan this event.

The Christmas Eve program was scheduled to start at 11:00 pm sharp. I was to meet the Praise and Worship team an hour earlier so as to have sufficient time to set up the audio-visual equipment as well as a last minute rehearsal.

At ten o'clock on the dot, I arrived at the school. Some of our equipment was stored there, the rest was with us. I had rented the school's gym recently for church.

I saw the Praise and Worship team pulling up at the same time in another car. I smiled widely. They were smiling widely. I could feel the Holy Spirit smiling widely too. Everything was going as planned.

"Merry Christmas!" I shouted. "Let's get set up! We have only one hour."

Credinescu and four others got out of their car, equipment in tow. "Merry Christmas! This is going to be great! We are so excited."

"Let's go!" I said, leading the charge.

We marched in through the rusted back gate of the school which was hanging precariously on its last remaining hinge. We could have avoided the gate altogether as the walls surrounding the school had fallen down upon itself leaving gaping holes the size of small cars. I wondered when the school would get around to fixing its decrepit perimeter. It was an eye sore and sure to turn off church visitors. But before my mind had time to dwell on this gloomy picture, Credinescu and his team burst out into song. Hearing the carols made my heart leap for joy again. We approached the gym.

"Wait here a minute. I have to get the keys," I said, indicating the guard house which was about fifty meters away.

I walked to the guard house and knocked. I could sense one naked light bulb glowing feebly through the grimy frosted windows. There was no response. I knocked louder. There was still no response. I rubbed at the glass and tried to peer through the frozen glass panels. It was useless. I might as well have tried peering through permafrost mud.

The thought that my carefully laid out plan was going awry rose up in me. I shook my head and quickly brushed off the sensation. My simulation model was perfect. Nothing could go wrong. The guard had to be in. I had spoken to him a few days earlier and had reminded him of the upcoming Christmas Eve program. He had been most cooperative then.

Credinescu, being curious as to my inexplicable delay, materialized at my side.

"What's wrong? Where are the keys?"

"This may sound stupid but I cannot find the guard," I said. "I knocked and knocked but nobody answered."

"Let me knock," Credinescu offered. "You probably knocked too softly."

"As you please." I made room for him.

Credinescu banged on the door with his fists loud enough to make all the stray neighborhood dogs start to bark and howl. Requited with the same absolute silence from inside, he started tugging at the door handle. The whole guard house shook like an elephant with the ague as he pulled and banged.

"You might want to keep it down a bit," I suggested. "We don't want the police coming here to find us breaking into the guard house. The guard may have gone out for a walk. Let's give him a few minutes."

"In this temperature?" Credinescu looked at me incredulously. "The guard would never do that."

"How would you know?" I asked confidently. "Let's wait for awhile."

We waited for fifteen minutes while the cold crept up our pants and coats. I could feel my organs shrinking.

Credinescu got impatient and started shaking the door violently. That got the neighborhood dogs howling like mad again.

"He's not here," I said, irritation creeping into my voice. "No point in shaking the door when he's not here!"

"What's your plan then?" Credinescu asked.

"I have the home phone number of the school director. We can call him. He may have a set of spare keys. Hopefully, he can come and open the gym for us. After all, I rented the space from him."

"Give me the number," Credinescu replied. He dialed and spoke tersely into the mouthpiece. The wind whipped away any snippets of conversation I was hoping to overhear.

"Did you get him?" I asked impatiently.

Credinescu turned around. His face was too frozen for me to read. "Well, he's at home."

"So? When is he coming?"

"He's not coming. He said the guard has to be here. Furthermore, he said he's the director of the school and it is not his business to open doors. And even if he was not the director of the school but just a guard, he still would not come on Christmas Eve as he is busy with his family."

I was shocked. "Are you sure that was what he said?"

Credinescu handed me the phone. "Do you want to talk to him?"

I shook my head. "That doesn't sound good at all. Well, no point in standing around here. Let's go and take a look at the door of the gym. It may be a simple process to get in."

We walked back to the gym entrance.

"How are you going to do it?" Credinescu asked curiously.

I was curious too as I did the mental calculations. A thick iron-grill door set in concrete was the first barrier. This grill door not only had a gigantic padlock but it had the added twist of a circular steel shroud ensconcing the padlock. I had never seen such a shroud before. Behind the iron-grill was a locked wooden door. That was the next barrier. Behind this wooden door was a short passage leading to a second locked wooden door. Behind this door was the gym. As some of our equipment was stored outside the gym, which abuts the school, we would have to break out of the gym, after breaking in, to enter the school itself. This was through another solid steel padlocked door.

I scratched my head. I could envision the layout of the school after that door. A mere three feet in, there would be another steel door. This second steel door would give way to a long passage which would end at a double steel door. Behind these double steel doors was the room holding our equipment. It was going to be like busting into a prison only to be confronted by a tank.

"It's not going to be easy but we can do it," I said faithfully.

"Maybe with many sticks of dynamite," Credinescu muttered.

"Quiet! Let me think."

Credinescu mumbled something else unintelligible but sounded equally disproving.

Suddenly a thought came over me. "I have a big screwdriver in my car. I can force this first padlock."

"Isn't it illegal to break into a building?"

"Technically, we are not breaking in. I have paid for this space and I have a right to use it."

"But you are still going to break the lock."

"Yes, but I will buy a replacement lock for the school next week."

Credinescu nodded his head. "Sounds acceptable."

I quickly retrieved the big screwdriver from my car. The leverage it offered would surely break the padlock, I surmised.

"Here goes!" I said, inserting the tip of the screwdriver between the shackle or the 'U' shaped metal and the padlock body. One big heave and the screwdriver snapped in two.

Credinescu nearly died of laughter.

My heart hammered in my chest as I looked at my watch. It was 10:30. I looked around the courtyard. About twenty people from the community had already gathered in the school courtyard. There was no time to lose.

"Credinescu! Do you have any hacksaws for metal at home?"

"Yes I have – several of them! Do you intend to saw through the shackle?"

"Five minutes and I will be through!"

Credinescu lost no time. He rushed to his car and shot off in a blast of snow. Fifteen minutes later he was back with the hacksaws.

That led me to my present predicament. I cast an exasperated glance at the shroud and rubbed my face with my palms.

"Yes, we will be here until next Christmas," I repeated. "I cannot get past this metal shroud!"

"How about the roof?" Credinescu asked. "Maybe it's easier that way."

"That will take a small nuclear device!" I replied in exasperation. "This roof is solid reinforced concrete encapsulated with permafrost. We are in Romania not Capernaum where the people lifted off the roof to get to Jesus. And I don't think any of us want another Chernobyl."

The crowd had now grown to about a hundred. I could read their thoughts. They were wondering why they had been invited and were now left outside to freeze like frozen meat carcasses. I could see the discontentment forming on their faces.

I peeled back my coat sleeve to peer at my watch again. It showed eleven. No wonder they were getting restive.

Frostbite will get you restive every time. The freezing rain was not helping either.

Then out of the darkness, Credinescu got an inspiration.

"We have car-jacks! Why don't we jack the grill-door out of its hinges?"

I quickly examined the hinges. "This grill abuts the concrete. If you lift up the door, it will hit the surrounding concrete. We have to lift the concrete as well."

"What do we have to lose?"

I agreed and we quickly maneuvered two jacks into position and started cranking. Less than ten seconds later the top of the grill hit the concrete.

"What do we do now?" I said, breathing heavily. "The hinges are not coming out."

"Let's continue cranking until something gives or breaks. These car jacks can take a whole lot more.'

We pumped the handles until the veins popped out of our arms. Then suddenly, the sound of concrete shattering and metal breaking rang out simultaneously in the night.

Credinescu was jubilant. "Look! We broke the hinges clean off!"

The grill door now hung by the padlock instead of its hinges.

"Quick!" I said. "Pick ten strong men from the crowd and let's bend this metal back on itself. That will allow us to get at the wooden door."

With muscles straining and sweat gleaming in the icy night, twenty hands started bending the steel door back on its padlock. The door bent about two feet but sprung back about a foot. The fresh coat of ice on the ground greatly hindered the metal bending process.

"That's the maximum we can bend this thing," Credinescu gasped. "People will just have to squeeze through this small opening."

"What about the wooden door?" I asked.

"No problem!" Credinescu backed about ten feet away from the wooden door and then rushed forward. With a flying kick, the wood splintered around the knob and latch. The door swung open. We were in the small passage.

Credinescu morphed into a Sampson-on-steroids. He rushed to the second wooden door. With a gargantuan pull he wrenched the whole door off its frame, throwing it onto the floor. We were now in the gym.

He flew across the floor to the metal door that gave access to the interior of the school. With strong sinewy arms, he grabbed the handles and shook the door to and fro violently. The smaller padlock on this door did not stand a chance. It broke clean. The next few metal doors all fell the same way.

I was close behind Credinescu. We smiled at each other. I wondered whether I would still be smiling so broadly the next day as I mentally chalked up the expenses of replacing each door that we were tearing down so enthusiastically now.

But this was not the time to worry about tomorrow. We dragged out chairs and speakers and a veritable hive of activity cascaded down upon the gym. The musical instruments were rapidly set up.

As the frozen bodies started dragging themselves in from the outside, Credinescu sidled up to me.

"Some of the bigger people cannot make it through the metal grill door!"

I looked up in amazement. "Why don't we get a few people to hold back the grill as these people squeeze through? Just make sure they do not let go of the grill too soon. We don't want people whacked with an iron door on the way in."

"I'll see to that!" He rushed off and came back with good news.

"We managed to get them in. Unfortunately, some had already left."

"We can't help that," I replied. "We will soon be done setting up the equipment and then we can get on with greeting the people and starting our service."

"Do you feel cold?" Credinescu asked.

"Of course I do!" I said, testily. "We just spent about an hour and a half outside in the freezing rain. Wait a few minutes and we will warm up."

"That's not what I meant," Credinescu said. "You may not have noticed this in all the excitement but this gym is frozen solid. Look at the floor – it has ice poking up under the wood!"

I looked at the floor unbelievingly. But Credinescu was right – a solid sheet of ice had infiltrated the floor and was now pushing its way upwards.

"How did this happen?" I asked, pointing towards the walls of the gym. "Those big radiators over there should have kept this place reasonably warm."

Credinescu rushed over to the radiators and felt them.

"There's no heat in these radiators!" he lamented. "They feel colder than Ceausescu's tomb."

I scratched my head. "I just don't understand. The school director assured me that there would be heat. Maybe the radiators take some time to warm up. We just busted in. Give it another ten minutes and we will be warm as toast."

"You don't understand. I don't think there is any hot water entering the radiators. They will never warm up! It is colder in here than outside. We are surrounded by frozen concrete and a frozen floor. The city must have switched off all heat to the schools during the holiday season. This way, they save money."

It took a moment for my numb frosted mind to register. "You are probably right. We will just have to bear this out. But at least we are out of the ice storm!"

Credinescu's smile came back. "That's right. We should be thankful that we are inside."

"See! You just need to see the cup as half full and not as half empty," I said, as I plugged the amplifier into the wall socket.

BANG!

A mini explosion sounded from somewhere deep in the heart of the school and the whole gym plunged into darkness. Some girls in the crowd shrieked. A few boys hooted and shouted 'Merry Christmas'. They thought the blackout was intentional. As I stood in the pitch blackness, the smell of pungent smoke coming from burning junction and switch boxes wafted to my nose.

"What happened?" Credinescu screamed.

"Sounds and smells like something burning. Does anybody have a light?"

"We don't smoke."

"You're no help. Doesn't anybody have any matches?"

Nobody answered from the pitch blackness. Then I remembered I had brought matches. And the candles! That was a Godsend. I rummaged blindly through plastic bags until I found the matches.

"I know where the fuse box is," I said. "Let's go and take a look at it. Try to act normal and don't scare the crowd. It's their first time here."

We lit some matches and walked nonchalantly through the gym – all the while smiling like idiots - to the hall outside. Once out of view, we rushed and crowded around the fuse box apprehensively. Credinescu lighted another matchstick.

"It's locked and there is a heavy smell of something burning inside."

"Should we be worried?" I asked. "It's not going to burn the whole place down?"

"Don't worry. This is not like a wooden American house. This is a Communist built structure. It will stand forever. It will never burn."

"If you say so, although we could do with some heat! Well, without any electricity, we cannot operate any of our music equipment, microphones, or projector. Do you guys think that you can get through this program with just one acoustic guitar?"

"I can't feel my fingers in this cold but I'll try," Credinescu said.

"What do we do for light?" somebody chimed in. "That's more important. We can't just let everyone sit in the dark. What will they think?"

I racked my brains. "Wait! I have some candles with me. I was going to use it later but this seems like an opportune time."

"That's a great idea," Credinescu said, "Let's go light the candles."

We walked back to where our now useless equipment laid and addressed the shivering crowd.

"We don't know what happened to the electricity," I shouted. "But we have candles for everybody. I know it is freezing but maybe the heat from the candles will heat up this place and your heart too. You can think of it as a romantic Christmas!"

Since it was Christmas Eve, the crowd was forgiving. Some of them even smiled back.

"Quick!" I whispered to my group. "Light up some more matches and hand me those bags."

I dug in the bags like a hungry bear foraging for food, found the candles, and fished them out proudly.

"I bought fifty of these candles. We can cut them in half. That way, we will have a hundred. That should be sufficient for everybody."

In the match light, I looked at the faces surrounding me. But instead of looking pleased they looked sick. They were staring at the candles apprehensively.

"Why?" I asked. "What's wrong? Too few candles?"

Credinescu was the only one brave enough to reply.

"The candles that you have in your hands are for the dead! People use those yellow candles only at funerals. We are celebrating Christmas! Surely everybody will leave this place if you give them candles reserved for the dead. This is insane! How did we end up like this?"

I stared at the yellow candles in my hand. I had broken through five doors in my own rented church building, the inside of the building had turned out to be colder than a dead Communist-leader's tomb, the electricity had shorted out leaving all the instruments useless, fuse boxes were burning throughout the school, and I was holding candles for dead people in my hands. To top it all, I had more than a hundred people sitting in the dark. I sighed. It was then that I remembered the food and bottled drinks in the trunk of my car. I seemed to remember, from my childhood days, learning in school that water expands as it freezes and breaks through bottles...

I sighed deeper.

Yes, how did we end up like this?

Specifically, how did I end up like this?

2. The Naïve and The Fool are Close Brothers

It was a beautiful autumn day in New York. I was selling my house and was having a huge garage sale. Everything was going smoother than a salmon's belly when a beautiful blonde accosted me in an upstairs room. I had made the mistake of telling her why I was selling everything.

"That's the craziest thing you could possibly do!" the pretty blonde said, in a shocked and horrified tone. She shook her golden locks and stared at me. "Everybody from that part of the world wants to come to America and you are going the other way? Why would you want to do that? Only a mad man would want to do that."

I could see what was going on in her mind. She was imagining planeloads and shiploads of people from the former Soviet Republics and the former USSR shoving and fighting their way to get to the good old USA and one person, namely me, going against this inexorable exodus – to Romania!

She wrinkled her eyes in abhorrence. The wrinkles did not blot out the blue of her eyes which shone like the sky on a fine day. "So why are you going to Romania? It's really terrible there! I would never go there."

"Why?" I asked weakly. "Are you from Romania?"

"No!" she replied. "I'm from Ukraine. Romania is our neighbor and everybody is leaving that country! They even come to Ukraine although for what I don't know! Romania is a very bad country! There is nothing there! Can you give me a discount on this four-poster bed? $2000 is too much! I also like that black convertible BMW outside. Is it for sale?"

I opened my eyes wide and swallowed hard. I looked at the blonde pontificator and realized that on some level she was right. Logically it made absolutely no sense. Nobody would leave a dream house and expensive toys in New York to travel to Eastern Europe without some very good financial motivation or reward. I had none! All I had was the gentle call from the Holy Spirit. But I couldn't tell her that. She already thought I was mad. Telling her about the voice of the Holy Spirit would guarantee me internment in the state asylum, which was just a few streets down from where we were.

So I chose to smile at her stupidly. "How much do you think the bed is worth?"

"$1500 is my final offer for the bed," she said. "And I want that cherry-wood bed chest included in that offer!"

Suddenly, a male voice interrupted the blonde. "I will give you $1700 for the bed and $2000 for that King Louis fireplace. And I want that black Bimmer! Give me a good price and I'll take it today!"

The blonde eyed her competitor condescendingly. "What about that gold colored car in the garage? Is that cheaper than the BMW? I adore it. I cannot believe that you will sell that too!"

"I will give you $3000 for the Bose-Yamaha sound system," a shaky voice said from behind me. I turned around sharply and stared at a fossilized grandmother that stood no more than four feet tall. My sound system stood at five feet exactly. I wondered what she wanted with a few thousand watts of power.

"How much do you want for the baby-grand piano?" a little girl asked, from the doorway.

I looked at all the people that had invaded the three levels of my house looking for bargains. It was the garage sale of the century.

"Sold!" I shouted at the grandmother. "Make your offers now!"

The midget grandmother shoved the Ukrainian blonde and the man aside like paper dolls, clawed at the bed post and screeched at the top of her wavering voice. "$2000 for this king-sized poster bed!"

"SOLD!" I bellowed. "SOLD!"

The blonde stared at me in bewilderment from across the room where she had been shoved. I smiled back to let her know I knew exactly what I was doing.

3. Black Bear and One-Eye

Swiss Air flight LX15 from New York to Romania was uneventful. Sitting in economy class, I felt pretty good in God's promise that He had gone before me to prepare the way, was with me now, and would be with me. After all, how hard could the road ahead be if God had prepared it beforehand?

With all my worldly possessions sold to follow God's plan for my life, I shifted comfortably in my seat and dreamt that God would move mightily and that all of Romania would come under conviction and be saved. After all, hadn't I quit a very profitable job as a professor of Operations at a revered private college, and a very profitable business as a financial consultant? Not only that but I was moving out of America to a former communist country! Wasn't that a big enough sacrifice for God? Surely God would have noticed my faith, just as He had noticed Abraham's faith, and would open the floodgates of heaven to shower me with unimaginable blessings.

I had read in Christian magazines that God rewards men and women of faith with huge ministries and even with private jets! These men had sown and God had multiplied their seed a thousand times over. I had seen pictures of churches numbering in the hundreds of thousands and I had seen the jets that some ministers flew in. I smiled in my dream. Sowing a car and reaping a jet sounded pretty good to me. In fact, maybe God was working miraculously right now, as I was in the air, and gathering thousands of complete strangers, climbing over each other to greet the plane, even before it landed, clamoring to be saved. What a welcome and escort that would be! Surely a big God could do that small a miracle?

With that thought embedded in my brain I rested and dreamt peacefully until the stewardess announced our landing. I sat up eager to meet the crowds that God had already prepared to greet me at the airport. In my mind, I knew that God's plan was blessed, and as I was just stepping into His plan, I would be blessed too. My heart pounded with excitement as the engines of the jet shut down. This was it!

The doors of the plane opened and I stepped out bravely into the new world. Much to my dismay, no cheers of adulation and adoration greeted me. In their stead, a cold Siberian wind howled and flitted between my clothes - in search of contraband ideology and theology. I swatted at the wind and wrapped my clothes a little tighter around me. Like everyone else, I proceeded down the passenger stairs all the while looking in vain for the eager crowds waiting to receive Jesus Christ as their Lord and Savior.

Once on the ground, four soldiers in military fatigues, armed with Russian AK-47's herded the passengers like sheep to the terminal arrival doors. I glanced at their bony unsmiling faces. They did not look like they wanted to be saved. I jogged obediently along with the rest of the passengers, more because of the cold than the assault rifles pointed at me. This was definitely different than any other airport I had ever been in. Still, though, it was an escort!

A new thought struck me as I jogged. The welcoming crowds must be inside the terminal building itself! Maybe it was just too cold for them to wait on the runway. Yes, that was it. I smiled all the way to the doors.

The dream was quickly shattered as I entered the terminal. It was no bigger than the living room in the house I had just sold. Any similarities ended there as the terminal was about a century older, painted a tired yellow, and was clearly devoid of any embracing crowds. My fellow passengers quickly melted into the yellow walls and grey wind. That left me alone to the curious appraising eyes of the soldiers.

In New York, I had arranged for transportation and accommodation once I landed in Romania. I thought it would be easy to recognize my driver. However, as I stood in the middle of the terminal, I soon realized that I had no idea whom I was to meet nor how I would be able to recognize him. Before I had time to figure this out, my driver spotted me, grabbed me and hurried me into a van. The van was black but I could still see the huge rust spots on it. My driver turned the key, stamped on the gas pedal and we shot out of the airport. I clung onto the threadbare seat for dear life. The driver swerved madly through the streets, avoiding pot holes the size of craters, along endless drab back roads and even drabber grey blocks of concrete buildings.

I cast an anxious glance at my driver. His face was a mask of concentration, his body bent stolidly over the steering wheel, as he drove like a possessed man through the dark streets. By some miracle, we did not kill any pedestrians or wrap ourselves around a tree. The van finally jerked to a halt in front of a humongous concrete structure in, what I was to find out later, the second worst neighborhood in all of

Romania. I was escorted and then left on the fifth floor of the structure.

There I met my landlord - a man blacker than night itself : black shoes, black pants, black belt, black pullover covered by a thick black leather jacket with black fur on the collars, black eyes, black bushy eyebrows that met and covered his whole forehead and short oily jet black hair. In the middle of all this blackness a very white, with an almost cadaver like sheen of hepatitis paleness, face peeped through. He resembled a bear and when he spoke his voice had a rough gasping throatiness that I thought Hollywood had invented.

"Beautiful place, no?" Black Bear said, showing me the flat. "Plenty space to sleep."

I looked around the cage, looked at his face, and nodded in silent acquiescence.

A black paw was thrust in my face. "Three months rent in advance. Six hundred dollars."

I parted with the money.

A toothless grin appeared as the money exchanged hands. A waft of alcohol, strong enough to knock over a very large draft horse, wafted to my nostrils. He pulled at my sleeve. "Come with me. Administrator here."

"I don't understand," I said.

He answered by pulling on my sleeve roughly. "You come."

I followed him out of the apartment door, crossed the landing, and found myself in front of a metal grill. Behind the metal grill was a solid oak door that appeared to have three locks on it. My landlord sunk his paw into a doorbell made from two exposed wires and smiled at me benevolently. I thought he would be fried to a crisp by the live wires but he seemed unaffected. Maybe his fur insulated him. He saw me looking at him and his smile widened. It was exactly like the look I thought a bear would have finding an unexpected stash of honey. I gulped. He said something unintelligible to me. It sounded important but I could not for the life of me figure out what it was.

I could hear bolts and locks being shot back. A few minutes later the oak door was thrown wide open. A blast of hot furnace air shot out.

Following the blast of hot air, a squat, hairy man emerged. Except for his blue underwear, he was completely naked. He looked like an overstuffed Hefty garbage bag that had a blue slit in the middle. Behind him, a squat woman of equally hefty proportions, and hair plastered with sweat appeared. All she had on was a pink bikini. In her hand she held a broom. I blinked and stared - wondering whether I was suffering from some type of wild jet lag vision impairment. The couple seemed real enough.

Black Bear and the Administrator exchanged a rapid torrent of greetings that sounded like they were shouting at one another. After some exaggerated hand gestures, Black Bear shoved me forwards as I was some type of gift offering. Administrator unlocked the metal grill door and shuffled closer. His wife stood unmoving, clutching the broom like a weapon, and eyed me suspiciously. The Administrator peered at me through thick glasses. That was when I realized that he had only one eye. I decided to name him One-Eye.

One-Eye adjusted the glasses on his nose and peered at me closely. He said something which I did not understand. I smiled like an idiot trying to appear friendly. One-Eye grabbed some papers off a shelf and wedged them between my hands. He tried to explain something to me. Black Bear nodded bearishly in agreement. I nodded along amicably, agreeing to gibberish which I did not understand, and all the while keeping a wary eye on the broom-wielding, scantily clad woman who had not spoken a word during this whole meeting. As we concluded our business, I was ushered back to my new place by Black Bear.

"You want drink after long trip?" he asked. "Bar is downstairs."

"No thanks," I said.

"You want girls?" Bear smirked. "You come here for girls. Romania girls most beautiful in the world! I get you girls for tonight."

"Uh, no!" I stammered, shaking my head. "I'm a Christian."

"No problem! I Christian too."

"That's not what I meant."

"Ah!" Bear nodded understandingly. "You tired. I get you beautiful girls tomorrow night. How many do you want? Three? Four? No problem."

I was too tired to answer. "Give me your number. I will call you if I want something."

"No, you cannot call me."

I pointed to the phone. "Yes, I can."

Bear shook his head. "Only for people calling in, not out. You sure you don't want drink? I am thirsty."

After I assured him that I really did not want any, we parted company. I had time now to examine the place I had just rented. I guess you could call it Eco-friendly for it was the greenest apartment I had ever seen. The walls were dark green, the furniture - consisting of two recliner chairs which did not recline - were a peculiar bright green, the doors were forestry green, the exposed pipes were painted green, even the phone was a slimy green. I felt like an ecological worm in a lime.

It was then that I realized that there was no bed in the flat. As I did not have a normal phone, I could not call Bear to question him about the missing bed. I ended up joining the two bright green recliners together and making a bed out of them. With my legs sticking up and out, I settled down for the night, I tried to look over the papers that One-Eye had given to me. As it was not in English, it made absolutely no sense to me and I gave up after a few minutes. It would have to wait for tomorrow.

It was my first day in Romania.

4. Mrs.Urdescu, the Communist Spy

Mrs. Urdescu was no beauty. She was as broad as a closet and had a face not unlike an English bulldog that had been caught red-handed downing a bottle of rancid vinegar. Something of a permanent lop-sided sneer was glued to her face. Her lips were nonexistent which complemented her pale wisps of unkempt hair, often bundled up untidily at the top of her head. She was a former Communist informant and she lived one floor beneath me. The next morning, she literally ran over me.

A jarring buzz had awakened me from my deep sleep. I stumbled all over the strange apartment looking for the source of the buzz before I found out that it was the doorbell. I opened the door and all of Mrs. Urdescu flowed in. Before I could blink, her sour dough face, her huge breasts, and her bigger stomach pushed me into a corner of the hallway.

"Yes?" I said, feebly, as I gasped for air. I was faintly aware that a strange woman had barged her way into my home uninvited and had trapped me with her breasts and stomach.

Mrs. Urdescu eyed me suspiciously and with great hunger. She spoke some English. Her eyes ate up the unopened bags in the living room.

"So you made all that noise moving in yesterday!" she said.

"I am sorry but I did try to be as quiet as possible," I said.

"People here sleep at night," she said accusingly. She poked her face in to the kitchen, scouting for clues. "We cannot sleep with noise."

I didn't know what to say. Right then, I didn't even know who she was.

She didn't find what she wanted in the kitchen and started moving towards the one remaining room of my two bedroom apartment. Her eyes scoured the hallway clean. She was still uninvited but I moved along with her as I was still caught between her breasts. "Where are you from and what are you doing here?"

I tried to extricate myself. "I am a missionary-pastor from New York."

"A what?"

"I am…"

Right then, I was saved from answering Mrs. Urdescu by the sudden appearance of my landlord, Black Bear. He had a huge loaf of brown unpackaged bread wedged under his sweaty right armpit. He must have sensed something wrong when he saw the open front door. Immediately, he started shouting at Mrs. Urdescu.

Mrs. Urdescu forgot about the last room and switched her attention to Black Bear who looked black as truffles, but of the imitation, not the expensive, variety. She shouted back at him as she flowed in his direction. I inhaled deeply as I escaped the many folds of her breasts. I presumed that the shouts were about me. Black Bear growled back threateningly. Mrs. Urdescu frowns grew until the bun at the top of her head burst. Pale blond hair escaped like lifeless seaweeds down her face. She did not notice it as she continued shouting malevolent threats at Black Bear. Then with a last threatening wave of her gelatinous hands, she stormed out of the flat, went down one floor, and we heard a door slam violently. The sound shook and reverberated through the whole building.

Black Bear turned around to face me.

"Communist spy!" He made a slashing gesture across his throat. "They should all be killed! Why did you let her in?"

I swallowed. "I didn't. She just walked right in. Who is she? What did she want?"

"The usual. Everything! She wants to know everything. But I told her nothing! We talk, eh?"

After we had settled into the lime green furniture, I managed to obtain a little more information from Bear.

"Big ugly woman, her name is Mrs. Urdescu, is Communist spy. You find one in every building! I spit on them!"

He spitted on the floor to show his disgust.

I gazed at the spit and nearly reminded him that I had rented the place from him.

Black Bear was in the mood for sharing. "Former Ceausescu's spies are everywhere. They live in the flats beside, above and beneath you. They listen through the walls, ceilings and floors. They go to school with you and they eat with you. They are your friends and they are your barbers. They play chess with you and visit your family. And then you disappear one night! Do you want some bread?"

I politely declined the organically armpit-salted bread as I took in my first history lesson of Romania. From what my landlord told me, I learnt that Romania was under communist rule from after World War II till 1989. Ceausescu became their leader around 1965. To control the population, he forcibly moved the rural population to large urban areas where they were contained in huge, grey apartment blocks. This proved both efficient and effective.

Efficiency was gained as Ceausescu's secret state police agency, the Securitate, recruited vast numbers of informers or spies whose job was to spy on their friends, neighbors, and work colleagues. Mrs. Urdescu, according to Bear, was one of those spies. Her job was to monitor movement of all residents in the block and report any suspicious behavior back to the Securitate – especially if a foreigner arrived and mingled with the locals. According to Bear, in addition to neighborhood spies, there were spies in academics, spies in theaters, spies among priests, spies among sportspeople, spies who spied on other spies, and child spies who spied on parents, teachers, and their friends in school. The children were the easiest to recruit as children could easily be blackmailed to rat on his or her friends. About 15% of all informers were children in Ceausescu's time. Families who listened to Western radio broadcasts or joked about Ceausescu would disappear in the night. Sometimes spies would be sent abroad to spy on dissidents living in other countries. The Securitate were so effective that Ceausescu became the most feared leader in the whole Eastern Bloc of nations.

"But why would ordinary people spy on each other?" I asked during one of Bear's pauses.

"Who wouldn't?" Bear replied. "You get reward, maybe some more food." He tore some chunks out of the bread, popped it into his mouth, and chewed on it vigorously.

"I don't understand. Some more food?"

"Let me explain," Bear said between mouthfuls. "Ceausescu didn't just build these hermetically sealed hellholes and then stop. He continued building."

From Black Bear's story, monstrous industries were then created around and for this contained population to maintain a sense of purpose and work. Here in these inefficient and ineffective industries, the people would pretend to work and Ceausescu would pretend to pay them. As time passed and more people were moved to the cities, the industries became grossly bloated with an underutilized workforce. As Ceausescu began to arbitrarily demand higher production quotas, the supervisors would lie and puff-up their figures of production. These imaginary numbers would then be covered up by the managers. The state, who managed the managers, would then lie to the whole country about these production figures. Mass lying not only covered up gross inadequacies but kept Ceausescu happy as well.

At the same time, the unmotivated rural workforce, their numbers drastically reduced by forced relocation, began to produce less and less food. Then in the 1980's, during the worldwide energy crisis, Ceausescu embarked on a mission to pay off the national debt. Energy, food, and natural resources were earmarked for export only. Consequently, there was not enough food left for the population and they starved. Also, about 95% of locally produced electricity was exported. Gas went the same way. This left the population in the cities sitting in the cold and dark and waiting six to eight hours in line to buy a loaf of bread or half a stick of butter.

"We used to say that Hitler killed the people by turning on the gas and Ceausescu killed the people by turning off the gas!" Black Bear grumbled.

"Maybe gas kills," I muttered darkly.

"So you get reward of food if you inform on your friends, your neighbors, your teachers! You will do it too if you are starving to death!"

"What about Mrs. Urdescu then?" I asked. "Maybe she did it for food."

"Not that woman! She is Russian and is Communist in her blood. That pig would inform for nothing! Greedy pig! She wanted to know what I got as rent money!"

Then to my amazement, Black Bear unsheathed a knife from his pants. It was about nine inches long and the blade glowed green reflecting the green décor of the apartment.

"I would slit her throat one day! Greedy ugly woman! What you say?"

I didn't know whether to agree with him or feign stupidity.

Black Bear laughed. He put away the knife back in his pants. His face turned sheepish.

"I want to ask you something," Bear bleated.

"What?"

"Can you give me another 3 months' rent advance? I don't have any more money. That is why I am here today."

I didn't want to say 'no' to a man who carried a nine inch knife in his pants.

"Come back in 2 weeks and we will see," I said, weakly. "I may have some money then. I will try to call you."

"You good boy!" Black Bear said. "I fix your phone for you. Stay away from evil woman downstairs. You want drink with me? I pay!"

"No thanks!" I wondered where he had conjured up the money for drinks so suddenly.

A thought struck Bear. "Maybe I can get your neighbor to come with me."

I was horrified to think that he would invite Mrs. Urdescu when he had so soundly and recently put her down. Black Bear must have seen the puzzled expression on my face.

"No, no." He made his fingers to resemble an eye and placed it on his forehead.

I got it. "Ah, you mean One-Eye! I am sure he would go with you but make sure that he put on some clothes first."

Black Bear did not understand what I was hinting at.

"By the way," I said. "One-Eye, I mean, the Administrator passed me some papers yesterday. What's it for?"

"Ah, you must register with police! And also border police. You must be on list. They track you. And also to pay all bills! Register to pay bills. Don't worry for now. I fix everything!"

He put his hands on my shoulders; bear hugged me, and then kissed me affectionately on both cheeks, the black bristles on his chin poking right through my skin.

"Remember, big ugly woman very bad!"

He laughed all the way to One-Eye's apartment.

ॐ

5. The Slaughter

"QEEEEEEEEEEEE!" The screams rose to an unnerving high pitch before subsiding. Then it started again. "QEEEEEEEEEEEE!"

I jumped out of the green chairs, now officially my bed, faster than a leopard from a tree, my heart racing and thumping painfully in my chest. I tried to pinpoint where the screams were coming from. It sounded like one of my neighbors was being murdered. Logic stated that it would surely be Mrs. Urdescu. She was done for this time. Her snooping days as a Communist informer were over. Her neighbors had banded together and decided to slit her throat.

Barefoot, I ran to the door of my apartment and put my ear against it. It was strangely silent. Quietly, I unlocked the door, tiptoed out and peeped out onto the landing below. I expected blood and gore but I saw nothing. It was eerily quiet. Where was Mrs. Urdescu?

Then the screams started again. It sounded like it came from outside. The neighbors must have dragged her outside. It was to be a public killing. I dashed back inside, rushed over to the windows and flung them open.

The wind burst in carrying with it a fresh salvo of screams. I held my breath, leaned on the sill and stuck my head out of the window.

I looked to my left, then to my right. I saw another few hundred curious heads, all leaning out of their windows. They were all gazing downwards so I followed the direction of their eyes.

To my relief, it was not Mrs. Urdescu. But it was a giant pink pig! Three men had attached a metal leash to a pig's neck and were dragging it out of a covered pick-up truck. I could just see its ears, head and front hooves as it struggled like a mastodon with its captors. The pig was so big and heavy that the pickup truck tipped up on its back wheels as the pig emerged.

With a thud the pig fell on the asphalt. The pickup truck righted itself with a clash of broken springs. A sense of victory swept over the three men and they must have breathed a collective sigh of accomplishment. It was a precipitous victory, for the next moment the pig had bounded to its feet and was rushing down the street pulling the men behind it. A collective gasp rose from the crowd still leaning out of the windows.

I watched with bated breath. The men dug in their heels and momentarily stopped the headlong rush-getaway of the pig. Quick as lightning, another man jumped out from nowhere and hurled himself onto the pig, tackling it to the ground. The pig and the man fell heavily - one on top of the other. As they rolled together down the street, the bright winter sunlight glinted off the glasses worn by this newcomer.

I recognized the man behind the glasses immediately. It was One-Eye! For a moment, there was a blurring distinction between man and pig as One-Eye was even rounder than the hog he was wrestling with. Eventually, man prevailed.

One-Eye seemed to have caught and tied the pig by its front legs. The other three men caught up, jumped on the pig too and immobilized its back legs. The pig squealed as if possessed.

Then One-Eye, still on the ground, produced a monstrous knife that could have killed a dragon, and in full view of thousands of pairs of eyes, jabbed with all his porcine strength straight into the pig's jugular. Blood spurted everywhere as the pig continued its valiant struggle against death. One-Eye repeated his action over and over again, each incision producing massive outpourings of blood. After a heroic fight, fit to put the pig into the Porky Hall of Fame for courage in battle, the pig finally succumbed and laid still.

The four men stood smugly over their prize. One-Eye laid down his saber-like knife, put his foot on the now dead hog and produced a bottle with a clear liquid inside. With a rowdy cheer the men downed the contents of the bottle in huge celebratory gulps.

I watched all this in fascination from my window.

The next few hours proved equally enthralling. After the mandatory alcohol feast, one of the men attached a hose with a burner to a propane tank. He lit the burner, adjusted the flame and then proceeded to light cigarettes from it. Each of the men took one. Puffing contentedly on their cigarettes, they then directed the flame at the pig. The hair on the pig lit up with a swoosh. In a short time, the skin was completely carbonized.

From under their coats, each of the men took out knifes and began scraping away the carbonized hair. As the hair fell off, I could see that the pig was no longer pinkish-white but a bright yellow. The flame thrower was then reapplied again and again until all that remained was a perfectly hairless pig. One-Eye reached for some snow and rubbed the pig with it until it was clean. Then he produced a shorter knife and with a masterful chef-stroke cut off the pig's ears, hooves, and eyes. The hooves and eyes he threw to a waiting pack of stray dogs. The ears disappeared into his mouth. Chewing on the ears happily and smiling broader than the Pillsbury dough boy, One-Eye then sliced off the pig's feet.

Next, One-Eye produced a medieval looking axe that looked like it had been taken off the body of Goliath. He adjusted his glasses, peered out from his one good eye and swung. He continued swinging until the pig was hacked into pieces. Still red with blood, the pieces were then carried into the building where I presumed that they would be salted or smoked.

As I continued to watch, a big pot was produced. The internal organs of the pig, mixed with handfuls of rice and spices were thrown in and brought to a boil. A smell fit for a king wafted upwards. When this mash was fully cooked, it was stuffed into the pig's own intestines and miles of sausages were extruded. The smell that rose up to my nostrils was heavenly.

My stomach rumbled in desperation. I felt light headed as I left the window. I had not eaten for a few days now and seeing all that pork and sausage made me realize how hungry I was.

Even at the risk of meeting Mrs. Urdescu on the staircase - and I knew she was lying in wait for me - I was going out to buy some food. I was not going to starve to death my first week in Romania.

6. Gypsies

"So you are carrying counterfeit money!" the first policeman said, suspiciously.

"Do you know that we can throw you into prison?" the second policeman snarled.

"We will teach you a lesson for coming into our country with counterfeit money!" the third policeman growled, swinging a gruesome stick that could have knocked out a rhinoceros.

The fourth policeman opened his jacket to show me his gun. It looked bigger than a cannon.

My throat was too dry to gulp so I just stared wide-eyed at the four grim-faced policemen that had encircled me. I didn't want to end up in jail, be beaten with a tree limb, or be shot full of holes. My stomach was the cause of all this trouble. I had succumbed to the vision and smell of pork and sausages. It had made me salivate worse than Pavlov's dogs. For some time now, I had survived on the organically salted, armpit flavored bread that Black Bear had carelessly left behind.

After the pig butchering incident, I had thrown on my casual suit, shoulder bag, Italian shoes and had ventured out of the apartment. I caught a meandering bus which took me to the city center. I had not taken more than a dozen steps in the middle of a busy street when I physically bumped into the four men. They were dressed in normal street clothes.

"Excuse me!" I said.

They did not budge. Two of them stood stalwartly in front while two went behind me. I felt like a sheep cornered by wolves.

I sidestepped but they moved in step with me.

"What's the matter?"

"We are the police," the first man said, "Where are you from?"

"New York," I replied.

"Have you been here long?"

"Not long – just a few days. Is there a problem?"

"No problem. We are inspecting foreigners. Our city has been flooded with counterfeit money carried in by foreigners."

"Counterfeit money?" I asked, in surprise.

"Yes. Foreigners have been caught trying to buy products with false money. We have to inspect your wallet for any such currency."

"I am not carrying any counterfeit money," I countered. "Furthermore, if you are the police, where are your uniforms?"

"We are in plain clothes," one of them shot back.

I looked at the man carefully. A swarthy brown complexion but neatly dressed. I did not know whether to believe him or not but I did not want to contradict him either. Furthermore there were four of them towering over me.

"Show me your police badge then," I challenged.

The man dug into his inside coat pocket and produced a police badge. He let me read it. It was official looking and it read POLITIA.

"Here!" the man said, thrusting the badge into my hand.

It felt heavy in my hands. This badge was definitely not from any Dollar-store. I handed the badge back gingerly. "I assure you I am not carrying any counterfeit money."

"Then show us the contents of your wallet," the first man ordered. "You have nothing to be afraid of if you do not have any counterfeit money. We just want to check."

"I don't want to show you my wallet," I said.

"So you are hiding something!"

"I am not hiding anything!"

"Then show us your wallet," the man said, his tone turning angry. "Don't play with us!"

I did not know what to think but being a foreigner, I wanted to be polite. I fished my wallet out of my shoulder bag. I could feel their eyes drilling into me. I opened my wallet and let them peek inside. They saw a small wad of US dollars inside. That was when the others jumped in and I was shown a glimpse of the gun. It dawned on me that I could be in real trouble.

"It is not counterfeit money!" I protested.

"That is what you say!" the first policeman yelled. "Give us the counterfeit money now!"

"I am not giving you anything," I said and put the wallet deliberately back into my bag.

That infuriated them. The first policeman grabbed me by my lapels and breathed in my face. "This is your last chance. We can kill you. Give the money to us right now!"

"I am not giving you my money!" I said obstinately.

Without warning the two policemen standing behind me started pummeling me with their fists. The one with the club raised it above his head.

I did not wait. I twisted myself out of the first policeman's hold and bolted down the busy street. All in one accord, they ran after me.

With my heart hammering more from want of breath than fear, I darted in and out of the swirling human traffic. I glanced back once and saw that the men were catching up. My Italian shoes hurt me. They were not made for running. Then without thinking, I dashed into a women's fashion store. I busted into the store so fast that I nearly took the glass door and a sales assistant down with me. The assistant stared at me like a deer caught in the headlights of an oncoming truck.

"Help!" I shouted at her. "Call the police!"

She continued to stare at me - standing like a piece of petrified wood. Her senses must have been numbed. I grabbed her by the shoulders.

"Call the police! THE POLICE!"

It was then that I realized that I was asking her to call the police while running away from the police! It did not make any sense.

From behind a sales counter, another woman appeared - tall, matronly, and dressed in a severe grey.

"What do you want?" she shouted at me.

"Call the police!" I begged, pointing to the door. "There's some people after me."

The tall woman walked out from behind the counter. She shoved her still petrified assistant aside and went to the front door to peer out. The four men were waiting a few feet outside. She turned around to face me.

I was visibly shaking now, trying to calm my labored breathing. Thank God I had run into the store. It was a tiny store but at least it was a refuge. I looked expectantly at the woman.

"We don't want trouble here," she said. "I want you to get out of my store!"

"Those people outside are waiting for me!" I protested. "Just call the police. That's all I ask."

"You get out of here!" the woman yelled. She walked towards me, flailing her arms and trying to shoo me out. "JUST GET OUT!"

I looked at her menacing attitude and concluded that I had made a mistake coming into the store. I crept towards the door, away from the woman, and surreptitiously peeked out from behind a curtain. The four men were still outside, trying to look nonchalant. Every so often they would glance at the closed door.

Right then, I saw a large group of people walking past the store front. This was my chance.

I yanked the door open and ran like the wind down the street, the passing group providing a temporary shield for me. The men, caught unawares, took a few seconds to realize I had escaped. They broke from their feigned nonchalance and gave chase.

Pounding down the street, curious stares came from all directions. I reached some street vendors.

"Call the police!" I gasped.

The street vendors took one look at me, the four burly men advancing like rockets behind me and shouted, "Gypsies! Bad people! Run! Gypsies! Run!"

I needed no second urging and ran for my life. I felt like Forrest Gump. Amid the hullabaloo and confusion of so many voices, I sprinted down the road towards a tram that was just pulling away from its stop. With all my strength I flung myself on board the departing tram as the doors closed behind me. I had no ticket and I did not know where the tram was going but I did not care. I was just glad to get away. Breathing heavily in relief, I made my way towards the back of the tram and gazed out of the back windows.

To my horror, I saw that the four men were still after me, only now they were chasing the tram. It was exactly like in the movies. They were pushing people to the left and to the right in their hasty pursuit of their prey. I must have been important to warrant such Herculean effort on their part. I watched transfixed as they ran on the sidewalk parallel to the tracks of the tram. I tried to will the tram to move faster, to lose the pursuing men. But it clattered on languidly, oblivious to my panting desires.

Then the tram started to slow down. It was reaching its next stop. With mounting terror I saw that the men were catching up. The tram had not even stopped when I punched the emergency button for the doors to open. The double doors clanged open stridently and I jumped out onto the street.

Without a backward glance, I ran across a busy road amid the honking of angry drivers. Some miracle prevented the cars from hitting me. I ran pell-mell towards a moving bus, grabbed the rails with my fingertips, and swung myself aboard. The bus picked up speed. It was only then that I afforded myself a backwards glance. I saw the men glaring angrily at the bus. Their dejected faces said it all - their prey with a small wad of US dollars had eluded them.

"Tickets please," a voice behind me said.

I turned my flushed face around to see an attendant. I did not know where I was heading but I had never been so happy to see a bus attendant!

7. Strugurescu and Baby Robbers

A few days later, Black Bear introduced me to one of his friends by the name of Strugurescu. He had a mop of curly black hair, alabaster skin, and was AWOL from the military. He was married with one son. Black Bear informed me that Strugurescu would help me around town in exchange for food, coffee, cigarettes, and English conversation. Or until the army found him. Before Bear left, he announced to me that he had connected my phone. That way I could finally call out.

I was glad to make the acquaintance of Strugurescu. After the incident with the counterfeit money, I was worried to paranoid about every person I met.

One of my first tasks was to make Strugurescu coffee. I poured a big mug for each of us as we settled in the green recliner chairs.

"Why do you have such ugly chairs?" Strugurescu asked.

"They came with the apartment," I replied stoically.

He looked underneath his chair and noticed sawdust leaking from it.

"Some bug is eating the chairs. If I were you I would throw them out from the balcony into the street. Do you have any sugar?"

I passed him the last cubes I had.

He tasted his coffee and made a prune face.

"This tastes like water after I wash my socks in. Don't you know how to make Turkish coffee?"

"I haven't had time to go out shopping yet," I said, not having a clue what Turkish coffee was. "Maybe we can do that today. I promise you stronger coffee next time."

At the same time I picked up my phone to check for a ringing tone. I started in surprise as a woman's voice came on immediately.

"Somebody's on my phone line!" I exclaimed. "Listen!"

The woman who had been laughing started shouting.

"I think she wants you to get off the phone," Strugurescu said. "You are disturbing her conversation."

I dropped the phone onto the floor.

"I didn't call her," I said in bewilderment. "Is it a bad connection? How come there's somebody on my phone line?"

"No, it's not a bad line. Bear gave you a shared line between two-three apartments. You can use the phone after your neighbors get off the line."

"You mean my immediate neighbors?"

"Not necessary. It can be anybody. They may or may not be your immediate neighbors."

"This is absurd. I don't want a phone where all my neighbors can listen into my conversations!"

"You probably have to wait a few years to get a private line," Strugurescu replied. "I have a friend who applied five years ago and he still has not received a private line yet."

"Five years!" I gasped.

"That's nothing," Strugurescu said. "Bear just switched on the phone for you. It probably took him two years just to get this shared fixed line. He probably also bribed someone to get this line."

"I will have to go to the Telecoms and see about this," I argued. "By the way, I have to go to the bank too. I need to get some checks."

"There are no Czechs in this country" Strugurescu said. "You can only find them in the Czech Republic."

"Not that kind of Czech! I mean, a check from a bank."

"Oh! That kind! No, we do not use checks as nobody trusts banks to pay on their demand. A little piece of paper is not going to be honored here. We only use cash which we carry around."

"I understand. But what happens if you want to buy something worth a lot of money?"

"Well, then we carry around big plastic bags to put all the money in."

"Forget it! Where can I find a bank to open up an account? Back home, I have an account with Citibank. Do you have a Citibank branch here in town?"

"Yes, we have. It is in the center of the city and just opened up a month or two ago. But it is not for you."

"What do you mean it is not for me? If it is a bank and I am a member then they must help me. Citibank is worldwide and have branches everywhere."

"I heard that they do not help people at all."

"That is ridiculous," I said. "Come with me and I will show you."

"Let me finish this brown water first. Are you sure you do not want to stop at a supermarket and buy some real coffee?"

"Maybe after the bank. Finish up and let's go."

The sun was shining brightly as we emerged into the street but it was still bitterly cold. Strugurescu informed me that we needed to change buses in order to reach our destination. We chatted about his work in the army as we waited for the first bus. He was a computer programmer for the military and had a comfortable sedentary office job. He was not required to do any morning exercises or partake in any operations. He told me that exercising just makes a soldier die healthier.

"Since Communism fell, there is nothing to do," Strugurescu said. "So I just sit around all day drinking coffee, smoking, and waiting for lunch and dinner. The computers I work with are old and slow, and they make mistakes. We were told that we would receive new ones soon so I look forward to making mistakes faster. This whole country is a big mistake. I would like to leave Romania one day. So I need to practice my English."

"That's fine by me," I said.

"Here comes our bus."

The first bus took us to the center of the city. From there we ran across a road to join a line waiting for the second bus which would take us to the front entrance of Citibank. Strugurescu told me that the second bus journey would take about five minutes.

After an interminable waiting time for which we could have walked to a nearby country, the second bus arrived. It rolled to a stop and its front and back doors creaked open grudgingly. Everybody, who a moment ago was standing in line, surged and pressed forward. It was free-for-all. Big men in winter polyester jackets trampled on us - they in turn were trampled upon by even bigger women in fur coats - as we all fought our way to the front doors of the bus.

"Get off my face," Strugurescu grunted to an old woman who was poking my friend in the face with a rolled up shopping bag.

"Look!" I shouted. "The back doors of the bus are open. Nobody seems to be getting on or off there. Let's get on the bus that way!"

We fought our way out of the mob and hurried to the back doors of the bus. There was a group milling around the wide open back doors but none of them were getting on. The bus was sardine packed at the back too but there was a small space left on the steps of the bus. I wondered why nobody was boarding. Strugurescu who was in front of me hesitated a moment and I stepped on him.

"Get up!" I yelled at him.

I pushed him in and managed to squeeze myself in behind him - just as the bus doors slammed shut behind me. We occupied the last step on the bus, our backs pressed against the closed doors.

"Whew!" I exhaled. "That was close. At least we got in."

Then I heard Strugurescu shouting loudly in front of me. Before I had time to react, Strugurescu pulled an Enoch before my eyes. One moment he was standing in front of me, the next moment he was not. He materialized again somewhere in the middle of the bus. My eyes bulged in puzzlement. What was happening?

Then I glanced up.

Right in front of, and surrounding me, were eight roly-poly, brightly garbed gypsy women. They all had babies or other small children slung around their necks, wrapped in a gay cloth. They looked like a happy family so I smiled at them. They smiled back, gold shining from their teeth. I was still wondering what had frightened Strugurescu so much when it happened.

With a concerted move, the eight gypsy women reached for me. Sixteen pairs of hands reached out simultaneously! It may be some men's fantasies to have that many women hands all over their bodies but it was definitely not mine. My heart stopped when I felt hands groping through my pants pockets, my shirt pocket, my two outside jacket pockets, and my two inner jacket pockets all at once. I could feel another pair of hands unbuckling my belt and unbuttoning my pants, attempting to pull it down! On my wrist I could see fingers prying at my watch. It was a surreal sensory feast unlike any other I had ever experienced.

I yelled and started beating off the hands. But my two hands were grossly mismatched to the sixteen that were all over me. The other passengers on the bus watched in silent fascination at the scene unfolding before them. A foreigner being undressed and robbed by a group of fat gypsy women in broad daylight on a public bus must be something new to them as well, for not one of them stepped forward to help. Or maybe they had witnessed this a million times before and were just bored.

My pleading eyes found Strugurescu's. He stared back wildly with a 'you-are-on-your-own' look. Now I understood why he had vanished so fast and why nobody had gotten on the bus through the back doors.

But I was not done for yet for I had a secret weapon hidden in a zipped inner pocket of my coat. It was a small canister of pepper spray that I had bought from E-bay before I left America. I reached for it.

That was when I saw something that made my eyes almost fall out of my head. Little brown hands were peeling back the brightly colored cloths that were slung around the gypsy women's necks. Adorable baby faces appeared next. Then to my dismay, the babies leaned over and their little hands began dipping into my pockets too.

"Help me!" I shouted at the top of my voice. "I am being robbed by babies!"

All thoughts of using the pepper spray disappeared.

Suddenly, the people in the bus came to life. A man being robbed by babies was the proverbial straw that broke the reticence of the crowd. With one accord, they started to shout and curse the gypsies. The bus driver, hearing the hullabaloo from the back braked sharply, throwing the gypsy women with their robber babies to the floor of the bus. As I had been braced against the doors of the bus, I was one of the few passengers left standing upright. I grabbed the opportunity and barreled my way through the fallen gypsies and their precocious babies to join Strugurescu in the middle of the bus.

The gypsy women, seeing their delicious foreign prey escaping, started shouting and cursing. The people on the bus shouted and cursed back some more. The bus driver left his seat, pushed his way to the back, and shouted and cursed at everybody. People started shoving one another. I stood there quieter than a church mouse in the middle of a wild buffalo in heat stampede.

A woman who was standing by my side leaned over and whispered, "Welcome to Romania."

I looked at her wildly. She seemed sincere but I was paranoid.

"Look!" I whispered to Strugurescu. "The front doors of the bus are open. Let's jump off!"

Strugurescu nodded. "Anyway, we can walk to the bank from here."

We burrowed our way to the front of the bus and hopped off. Then I made the mistake of glancing back at the rear doors of the bus. The gypsy women immediately saw me. More shouts ensued, the rear doors hissed open, and the gypsy baby-toting women burst out like a multi-colored tsunami. They ran towards us.

"Run!" I shouted.

Strugurescu took one look at the wild troupe of women and babies advancing towards him and his never-been-exercised legs suddenly found new power. We sprinted up the street ten times faster than the bus.

Then I saw Citibank! But it was on the other side of the street. Strugurescu, jogging by my side, was panting so hard that I thought he was going to explode and burst through his own skin. The bus, which had started up again, now ran parallel with us. The passengers inside were shouting out of the windows cheering and encouraging us on. I sneaked a backwards glance. The wild profusion of red, green, orange, yellow, and purple gypsy skirts were still hurtling inexorably towards us.

As we neared Citibank, I took a chance and ran directly in front of the bus. As I had expected, the bus screeched to a jarring halt. Like frightened jackrabbits we scooted past the bus to reach the other side of the street. The gypsy women struggled after us but were blocked by the bus which had started moving again. This gave us a minute of advantage. Breathing like overweight and under-exercised men, we ran up the steps, passed the huge glass doors, and into the safety of Citibank. Strugurescu collapsed in the lobby as the bank security guards rushed forward to confront us – probably with the thought that we were indubitably the most inept and out-of-shape robbers that they had ever seen.

"We need help," I gasped, pointing to the approaching colorful horde.

This time, my call for aid was heeded. Good-old corporate America training must have sharpened the security guards' senses. They rushed outside, guns drawn, to intercept the horde.

"Thank you!" I breathed to three smartly attired receptionists who had also rushed out to help us.

The gypsies, upon seeing the security guards, fled like a school of graffiti coated manatees in every direction. In the lobby of Citibank, Strugurescu and I tried to calm our labored breathing. I looked at the receptionists. They were smiling calmly at us. I asked to use the restroom leaving Strugurescu in the lobby holding his head in his hands muttering dark secretive threats.

I didn't know that being a missionary required so much running! Standing in front of the floor to ceiling mirror in the restroom, I checked the contents of my pockets to verify that I had not been robbed. I felt pretty confident that the gypsies had not pilfered anything due to my running away faster than a scared rabbit.

But to my consternation and dismay, I discovered that the secret inner pocket of my jacket had been picked. A little pouch that held my passport, driver's license, credit cards, and the Citibank card was missing. My heart stopped.

At that exact moment, Strugurescu pushed the doors of the restroom open.

"A woman found this down the street. She just came into Citibank and handed it to the security guard. The guard gave it to me to pass to you."

I stared in astonishment at the pouch that I had just discovered was missing. I grabbed it from Strugurescu's hand and rushed out of the bathroom.

"Where's the woman who gave this to you?" I asked the surprised guard.

"She left a second ago," the guard answered. "She should be outside if you want to talk to her."

I dashed out through the glass doors into the street again. I looked up and down the street but it was completely empty. There was not one person on the street! I went back in to talk to the guard.

"There's nobody out there!" I said.

"Impossible!" the guard sputtered. "This is a long street. She must be out there!"

In turn, he rushed out to look for the woman. He came back in again after a few seconds, shaking his head in wonderment.

"She's not there!" he said in a puzzled tone.

"I just wanted to thank her," I said. "She returned all my documents that the gypsies stole in the bus. The gypsies must have thrown the pouch as soon as they discovered that it had no money inside. Strange how she walked inside this particular building when there are so many other buildings on this street. I wonder who she was."

Nobody answered that question.

Then one of the receptionists spoke. "How can we help you?"

I pulled out my Citibank card. "I would like to open up a checking account please. It has been quite an adventure to just get here."

"We cannot open up an account for you," the receptionist said, still smiling beautifully.

"Why not?" I asked. "This is my Citibank account card from New York. This is a Citibank overseas branch. Here's my passport and my drivers license. What is the problem?"

"We cannot help you as we only serve corporations here in Romania," the receptionist replied cheerfully. "We do not serve individuals!"

I stared incredulously at the cheerful face.

"See!" Strugurescu said. "I was right. I told you that they would not help you here!"

☙❧

8. A Discussion on Gypsies

After the visit to Citibank and the failed attempt to open an account, we caught a bus back without any further incident. We stopped at a small local grocery store to stock up on essentials. I also dropped in at a second hand store and bought a Whirlpool washing machine. The salesman promised that the appliance would be delivered later in the week. As Strugurescu and I parted company outside my building we agreed to meet the next day for more conversations in English.

The next day, from my replenished provisions, I resolved to make coffee that would put some hair on Strugurescu's back. I was still smarting from his previous comments about my coffee. I was determined to show him that Americans could also make coffee that does not resemble 'water-I-washed-my-socks-in'.

I went all out this time. I must have used a quarter can of coffee. The end concoction was so strong that the spoon stood up without any help from the rim of the cup. I was convinced that it was powerful enough to knock over an adult bison.

As Strugurescu and I sank in the lime green chairs, coffee cups in hand, copious amounts of sawdust oozed onto the floor. At the present rate of ooze, I figured that I would have a small Giza pyramid in my living room by next month.

Strugurescu sipped his overbearingly strong coffee and commented on the weather perfunctorily.

"How's the coffee?" I ventured.

"This is good!" Strugurescu said, displaying his irreparably yellowed teeth. "Better than Turkish coffee. I see you've learned something here in Romania."

I waited for him to fall over but he must have had a constitution stronger than a bison. He stayed put.

I put down my cup of untouched coffee. I was confident that I was not as strong as a bison. "Yes, I did. Maybe you can teach me something else today."

"What would you like to know?"

"Tell me about the gypsies. I have had several encounters with them and I still don't know anything about them. We don't have gypsies in the States."

Strugurescu put down his cup reluctantly. "You are wrong. There are probably more than a million of them there. They first went over with Columbus as slaves in one of his voyage to the Americas. You cannot tell who they are because they can pass themselves off easily as Mexicans or even Native American Indians. Same skin color, you know. Unless they choose to tell you, you may never know."

"You are probably right. But where are they originally from and why are there so many of them here?"

"Let me tell you what I know. You have to go back many, many years. In about 1000 A.D. a band of warriors was formed by the King of India to resist the spread of Islam in Northwest India. This band was known as Rajputs and the King granted them special honorary 'warrior caste' status.

The original gypsies were either part of the Rajput warriors or worked for them as metalworkers, entertainers, cooks, or carpenters. However, the Rajputs were defeated, captured, and brought into the Byzantine Empire as prisoners of war. These prisoners than became slaves to the Ottoman Muslims. The Byzantine Empire is roughly where modern Turkey is today. Later, they moved into Europe, following the wars of their Muslim masters."

"Didn't they rebel?" I asked.

"If they rebelled, the Ottomans would cut off their lips, whip the skin off the soles of their feet, or roast them alive over a burning fire. Their females would then become sex slaves to their master or their masters' guests. I am sure that these actions greatly discouraged rebellion. However, the Ottoman-Muslim warriors were in turn defeated and pushed back from Europe. The gypsies who were left behind then became slaves to the Russians, the Romanians, as well as to all of the other countries where they had moved to with their former masters. They now became slaves to the crown, to the church, to the land barons and to other noblemen. They were valuable as these gypsy slaves were noteworthy in basket making, blacksmithing, knife-grinding, locksmith-ery, violin-playing and other general handyman tasks."

"So what you are saying is that the gypsies once started out at the top as warriors in India, but hundreds of years of slavery in foreign countries have reduced them to the bottom of the social and economic ladder."

"Yes, you got it," Strugurescu nodded. "The whites especially did not like their dark skin - equating black with evil. White was considered pure so the gypsies got a bum rap right from the start. Of course, the gypsies being from India had their own language, customs, and religion. This was often considered foreign and downright threatening to the white's Christian doctrines. Also, the gypsies used to shun intermingling with non-gypsies for they considered them unclean! This made them appear to be even more furtive, sly, and covert to their European masters."

"Wait!" I exclaimed. "You said that the king of old India gave the gypsies honorary warrior caste status. Maybe they took that to heart and considered themselves above the lower classes or castes or white masters. Not knowing the caste system would make the gypsies appear furtive and sly."

"You are probably right. That being said, as the gypsies had no nation, no military, no economic power, and no political voice, it was easy to perpetuate their slavery. It's like a self fulfilling prophecy. Treating them like animals over hundreds of years make them act like animals. Did you know that the Nazis called them carriers of the plague or excrement of humanity? They believed that the gypsies carried genes predisposing them to criminal acts. Therefore it was necessary and admirable to eradicate all of them. They began with compulsory programs to sterilize all gypsies. When you compare the black complexion of the gypsies to the lily white of the Aryan Germans...well, you can see why they were thought of as lower than excrement! White is pure, black is bad. At least a million and a half gypsies were exterminated at the Auschwitz-Birkenau concentration camps."

"I didn't know that. We hear a lot about the Jews being annihilated at these camps, but never the gypsies. Also, I believe that the Germans have publicly apologized and made reparations to the Jews, but nothing to the gypsies. Why do you think this is so?"

"Nobody cares about gypsies here in Europe. They are often the brunt of racist violence and discriminatory governmental policies. They are considered irreparable. As such they were banished into slums or deported to slums in other countries. They are outsiders and rejects without hope of redemption. Here in Romania, it is no different. Romanians, as a race, are the product of interbreeding between strong Roman legionnaires and the white European Dacians. The Dacians were the original settlers of this country from 2000 B.C. onward. The Romans conquered the Dacians in A.D. 101, making this region the frontier of their empire, intermarried, and then just simply stayed behind. However, they were all white! So as you can see, gypsies were never considered 'real' citizens. Why would the German government be an exception when every other country, including ours, thinks that way?"

"Why didn't the government try to integrate the gypsies into the community?" I asked.

"Which government? The German or the Romanian?"

"I meant the Romanian."

"They did try during Communist times. They forced the gypsies into apartments with other Romanians."

"How did that go?"

"Not well at all. The gypsies took their horses into the apartments. Then they dug up the parquet floors and used the wood to build a campfire in their living room. Their Romanian neighbors banded together and kicked the gypsies out. They are people whom nobody wants. They are the 'un-people'."

"That is not what God says about His creation," I countered.

"I know what the Bible says," Strugurescu said. "But the gypsies do not want God. They want a life free of moral constraints. Come to think of it, they want freedom from authority, responsibility, work, hygiene, and everything else. You cannot change a gypsy! What does your God say about that?"

9. Conversations with God I

The only way for God to draw close to us is for us to draw close to Him. I speak to God everyday and He speaks back. He speaks back to me mainly through scripture. He also speaks to me through a still, small voice that to this day amazes me in its clarity and supernatural wisdom. In my prayer time, I took up Strugurescu's question about the gypsies with Him.

"Father, what about the gypsies?" I asked. "Are they really useless?"

"In the kingdom of heaven, no one is useless. Everybody has talents even though they may not recognize it. These talents have to be discerned and then encouraged to grow to their full maturity. Gypsies are imbued with the idea that they are absolutely useless and have no talent whatsoever. In fact, they have been constantly told and shown since the day they were born that they were unwanted and inutile. Since society rejects them, they believe falsely that I reject them too.

In the parable of the laborers, the people hired early in the morning at nine o'clock are the ones most sought after. They are like shining stars. Their resumes are a head-hunters dream. They can do anything. They are the Olympians and the leaders.

The next group of people - those hired at noon and at three o'clock are the majority. They may not shine, but they have the capacity to work and persevere in life. They are the backbone of society, the middle class who carry the country along.

The last group of people are those whom society rejects. Those who cannot be employed because people think there is something wrong with them. They are still left in the marketplace at the end of the day. The poor, the uneducated, the weak, the ones who cannot find dates because they are too fat or thin, the ones whom other boys and girls shun and laugh at in school, the ones who made multiple mistakes in life, the alcoholics, the addicts, the losers, the bums, and those whose skin color is different. They are left behind because no one wants them. These are the true 'gypsies'. Wanted by none but yet are chosen by Me."

"Am I to reach out to the gypsies then?" I asked.

"I called you to be a light in the darkness. Not only to the gypsies but to the millions who are equally lost here. For the rich also need My Son, Jesus. Zacchaeus was rich but lost. But I entered his home and heart. Look at your hands for a moment. Do they only minister to the poor? Do you focus on the rebellious instead of the lost? Or do you try to reach the lost as I have called you to? Listen to your heartbeat for a moment. Does it beat only for a certain group of people? Does it beat in frustration trying to bring in someone else's harvest? Or does it beat in time with My heart for my lost sheep which I have called you to?"

"I will reach whomever You want me to reach," I replied.

However, it was easier said than done.

❧❧

10. Pigs Do Fly

After a couple of weeks of running around the city on foot, I construed one rainy morning that I was taking too much time accomplishing too few things. In fact, I was accomplishing nothing but running away from people whom I should be sharing Jesus Christ with!

My conclusion was that I needed a car!

"Where can I rent a car?" I asked Strugurescu. "I want to visit the Music Conservatory to put up an announcement."

"Rent a car?" Strugurescu sputtered. "Why would you want to do that?"

"Look at the rain outside. Furthermore, it takes too long to wait for buses and trams and it is not safe. I am certain I can do more if I can drive."

"Nobody rents cars here. It is just too risky."

"I'm a good driver. I won't get into an accident."

"No, you don't understand. People don't rent cars here because the renter will just steal the car. They will drive it to Russia, Ukraine, or Moldavia and sell it there."

I looked at Strugurescu. "You are joking, aren't you? You cannot just steal a car like that. You must have papers, like the title for the car."

"Papers can be bought easily. Sellers advertise car identification papers for sale in the local newspapers everyday. You can get them for a few hundred dollars."

"What about the border guards? Don't they check before allowing cars to drive through?"

"You are so naïve. Border guards are among the most corrupt in the country. They will turn a blind eye if you put a few hundred dollars in your passport and hand it to them."

"I can't believe that! Surely there must be some honest border guards?"

"It would be downright stupid to be honest when you can get away with corruption so easily. Who is to know if somebody slips them something?"

I couldn't argue with that. "OK, you win. I will forget about renting a car. Come to think of it - you have a car! Why don't you rent me your car for a few weeks?"

Strugurescu nearly fainted. "You want to rent my Traban?"

"Why? What's wrong with it? It's a car, isn't it? Like I mentioned before, I'm a good driver. I have driven for many years."

"I am trying to protect you!"

"Protect me?!"

"Let me tell you a true story about the Traban, the wannabe cardboard car made in former East Germany."

"Yes?" I said curiously.

Strugurescu leaned closer. "Well, there was this green Traban that was stopped at a traffic light. Alongside it came a horse and cart. As the story goes, the horse was hungry and seeing the green Traban, mistook it for grass and began to chew on the roof. Before the light turned green, the horse had eaten half of the roof!"

"You are kidding me?"

"I swear I'm not kidding!"

I shook my head. "Now I really must see this car and try it out. Look, I know you are trying to protect me but do you think you can allow me to drive it around the neighborhood? Just for a few blocks? I will make up my own mind after I have a go at it."

Strugurescu threw up his hands in frustration.

"Why don't you rent a Dacia – the local Romanian built car? It's much better than the Traban."

"I don't know anybody with a Dacia. I'll give you US$10 per day for your car."

Strugurescu's face contorted with conflicting emotions.

"I will think about it. But today, to go to the Music Conservatory, let's take the tram instead."

"OK, but just for one more day. Tomorrow please lend me your car."

We headed out of the apartment and into the street. The rain had stopped but the thick dust of the city had amalgamated with the rain to form a brown sludge. We squelched through several streets to a tramline that would take us to the Conservatory.

As we stood waiting for the tram, I could not help noticing piles of garbage strewn haphazardly all over the streets. Cans, bottles, cardboard boxes, newspapers, plastic bags, even some decrepit sinks were thrown without regard all over the road. To the right of the tram stop was a busy neighborhood wet market where hawkers congregated. Boxes of rotting vegetables and fruits, crushed beneath the feet of an unending stream of people added to the mess.

Directly in front of the tram stop was a 4-way intersection. Cars blared their horns at pedestrians as they trudged across the sludgy road. The pedestrians, in turn, shook their fists and glared angrily at the cars.

Through this cacophony of noise and general bedlam, traffic signs were blatantly ignored. I saw four cars squeezed into the two-lanes before me. As I watched, several other cars drove up and stopped in the middle of the road.

"Did you see that?" I asked. "That driver just parked his car on the road and walked away into the market. Now all the cars behind him are blocked!'

"That's nothing!" Strugurescu remarked. "Wait till you start driving."

I laughed. "Look at that small car over there trying to get around. It has at least ten occupants in it! That's a big family. Its muffler is scraping the road. And that other car has bales on top of it, four times its size! It looks exactly like a mushroom on wheels."

"That's how the sellers take their stuff to sell in the market. They don't have any vans or trucks. That overloaded car with all the people inside – that's not a family. Many people in this country do not have cars, so they hitch a ride and pay a token sum of money to the driver."

Suddenly, a small brown car pulled up at the tram stop directly in front of me, making a fifth lane from the two lane road. I was amazed by the appearance of a fifth lane - on the smooth tram tracks, but I was even more amazed by the occupants of the car.

All the seats, except the driver's, had been ripped out. Sitting beside the driver and in the back were about half a dozen pigs! They snorted loudly at me.

I stared unabashedly at the pigs and then at the driver. He did not seem perturbed. His focus was on the traffic lights.

The light finally turned green. All five cars dashed forward like mustangs at the starting line, the little car on steel tracks. With its exhaust spewing out a storm, the little brown car accelerated and shot through the intersection making a wild left turn. As it veered left, the car tires flew off the smooth tram tracks and hit the road hard. The four-inch difference in height between the tram tracks and the road caused the little car to shudder violently. Suddenly, one of the back doors of the small car flew open!

Literally, two pink pigs flew out of the car. My jaw dropped as the pigs slid out from the car. Time stood still as I watched the pigs fly in symmetric beauty. I watched the driver's mouth shouting noiselessly as his pigs escaped. I watched Strugurescu's eyes pop out of his head. I watched the rain fall on all of us.

Then with a splat, I was jerked out of my reverie, as the pigs landed in the middle of the busy intersection!

Cars screeched to a halt and pandemonium ensued. The flying pigs, unhurt, picked themselves up right away from the wet sludgy street. I could see the driver of the small brown car hurling himself backwards to pull the back door shut to prevent the other pigs from escaping. Traffic in all four directions grinded to a halt amid a bedlam of noise, shouts, honks, and squeals.

A crowd immediately formed and surrounded the intersection. The pigs stood still after their landing. Then, slinking between the legs of the curious onlookers, a pack of stray dogs, their hair still dripping from the rain, appeared.

Before anybody could react and without any warning, the dogs charged the pigs. The two pigs went hog wild and bolted - shrieking, squealing, and grunting as they slipped and slid on the muddy road.

The pigs made for the only opening they saw – the tram stop!

As I saw the pigs galloping towards me, followed by a pack of barking and gnashing teeth, I prepared myself for the prospect of being run over by the pigs, and following that, to be trounced by the dogs.

With a resounding howl of fear, the people waiting at the tram stop bolted in a spray of mud. I lost sight of Strugurescu as I found my legs and dashed for safety across the road and into the marketplace. I skidded and trampled on bags, vegetables, and bottles before hurling myself behind a kiosk. The roar of hoofs, paws, and heels thundered down the road past the market. Somewhere in the distance I could also hear police whistles.

Strugurescu found me after a few minutes.

"Are you sure you still want to go to the Conservatory today?" he asked breathlessly. "You look kind of muddy!"

"It can wait for tomorrow," I panted, picking myself up from the mud. "You never told me that waiting for a tram could be so dangerous! Now do you understand why I would like to drive?"

Strugurescu threw up his hands in despair.

"You win! I will drive my Traban here tomorrow and you can test it."

"I'm looking forward to it," I said. "Eight sharp! I'll be waiting. By the way, what was that driver doing with all those pigs disguised as passengers? It's not like there is a fast lane here."

"He was taking them to be slaughtered. In this country, a person raises his own pigs and then slaughters them for meat during the holiday seasons or when necessary. You cannot just go out and buy pork. Same for chicken and beef. It is called self-sustenance."

"I would hate to be in a car full of cows," I muttered.

"If you want beef, then you will do it," Strugurescu muttered back.

ಹ⊸ಣ

11. Adventures at Home

I was glad to be alive but disappointed that I was now not only running away from people but also from animals. I thought I must be the worst missionary in the history of missions!

I got into the shower to rinse off the mud. To date, I am astonished at the extremely poor urban planning of the bygone Communists. Concrete cities of a million or more people were completely devoid of greenery. In places where there should be parks or gardens were mountains of dirt and garbage. In the winter or rainy months, these mountains of dirt would become mountains of mud. It was an indescribable mess.

These thoughts filled my mind as I entered the tiny shower. Unlike the rest of the apartment which resembled a lime, the bathroom was once painted a jovial light blue. But mold and mildew had tampered the jovial blue to a greenish-blackish slime, which ran down the perimeters of the walls. A 100W bare bulb, with exposed wires, hung sadly over the bathtub. Its glare highlighted the wilted blue of the walls.

My landlord, Black Bear, must have fancied himself as a plumber; for no self-respecting plumber would have designed the shower the way this one was designed. Two thick rusty main pipes, one for hot water and the other for cold, jutted at right angles out of the concrete wall. Black Bear had managed to screw two rubber hoses onto the ends of these pipes. The two rubber hoses were then threaded together with a plastic connector to form a single hose, very much like a doctor's stethoscope. At the end of this single hose was a makeshift valve that opened or closed the water flowing to the rusty shower head.

I turned on the valve and stepped into the yellowed and cracked bathtub. The water was surprisingly hot, and under great pressure. Standing under the shower was akin to having a massage. I let the water run down my head and back. The brown mud, that caked my skin, made a small river as it drained away.

Just then, the unexpected happened! With a loud swoosh, the stethoscope hose snapped at the plastic connector point. The break was clean and smooth. No knife could have made a cleaner slash. The two hoses now freed from the connecting shower head jerked and danced wildly like two snakes having their tails stamped on. The water first shot down into the bathtub and then up vertically towards the ceiling. I barely had time to figure out what had happened when the light bulb above me exploded.

BOOM!

The shards of glass flew in all directions. A sudden chain of events took place rapidly. First, the water shorted out the exposed wires in the bathroom. Next, the century old Communist built fuse box located in the hall blew with a tired gasp and a strong wisp of smoke. An acrid smell filled the flat, as the whole place plunged into darkness.

Then through the concrete walls of my flat, I heard a resounding shout. Doors slammed, as yells of annoyance, frustration, and anger could be clearly heard. I froze. Then it dawned on me. The whole block's electricity must have shorted out. There were a few hundred flats in the block where I lived. That meant a few hundred families had lost their power. I wondered about other nearby blocks.

My mind raced as I stood naked in the bathtub trying to figure out what to do next. One thing was certain - I had to catch the thrashing, undulating snakes. The water was now pouring and raining on me from the ceiling. Glass was floating in the bathtub and on the floor. Like a cheap kung-fu movie, I reached out and wrestled with the two wriggling snakes. It was then that I realized that there was no way to switch off the water as the open-close valve was on the severed side. I released the hoses which immediately commenced their wild gyrations anew, like a whirling and twirling opponent - one moment spouting freezing cold water and the next boiling hot water at me. I wanted to laugh so badly but couldn't.

I needed to act fast. I also had to put on some clothes. But I could not move because of the shattered glass! It was a dilemma. The bathroom floor was fast becoming a swimming pool. I had visions of the floor collapsing. That would deposit the bathtub, a few thousand gallons of water and a naked missionary into Mrs. Urdescu's, the Communist spy, apartment below. That would truly be the end of the world for me.

Then I got my 'Eureka' moment. The bulb glass shards floated in water! As long as I did not lift my feet off the floor, I would be alright. I crawled out of the tub, my hands feeling the darkness before me. I finally reached the towel rack and the dripping wet towel.

The towel was not for me. I crawled back to the tub and threw it over the water hoses that were still spouting steam and water everywhere. I straddled the hoses in the dark and knotted them together with the towel. My adversary was subdued. The water now gushed into the towel, then straight down into the tub to be drained away.

Suddenly a loud pounding sounded on my front door. I jumped out of my skin as I had no clothes on. I crept silently to the front door and peered through the peep-hole. In the landing outside, by the light of a flickering candle, I saw One-Eye. The candle light bounced off his glasses accentuating his one good furious eye.

I fled.

I ran to my suitcases and quickly retrieved more towels and got dressed. I could clearly hear shouts in the landing now. I surmised that One-Eye was scouting around door-to-door trying to locate the source of the power outage.

I had to act fast. If the water seeped through the concrete floor to Mrs. Urdescu's place below, I would be discovered as the culprit. I felt around for a bucket before I realized that I did not have one. All I had was a round toilet brush holder!

Next moment, I was scooping water wildly with the toilet brush holder and emptying it into the tub. It was small and not designed for use as a bucket but I compensated by working like a madman in the darkness. After what seemed like an eternity, the water level went down to where I could use the towels to mop up the remaining puddles. I wrung out the towels in the tub. I began to breathe easier as the minutes ticked by and neither Mrs. Urdescu nor One-Eye materialized to wring my neck.

Back in the living room, I called Black Bear.

"Come quick!" I pleaded. "The shower just broke and I cannot stop the water."

Raucous music was blaring in the background. I presumed he was in some honey joint.

"Just close the valve," Black Bear shouted.

"The water is shooting out from the wall," I shouted back. "The valve fell off."

Black Bear did not appear to understand the urgency of the matter.

"I'll be there in three days time," he bellowed into the phone.

"What am I suppose to do in the meantime?" I replied.

"Relax! And take a drink!"

And then Bear hung up.

I prayed for morning.

⤦⤧

12. A Dog's Life

The next morning, I showed Strugurescu the still flowing broken shower.

"I can't turn it off," I said. "The owner told me he would be here in three days time!"

Strugurescu took a cursory peek at the pipes.

"Why don't you shut the main pipes off in the basement?" he asked.

"I didn't know that you could do that," I said.

"Yes, you can do that. If somebody's pipes break, that's what they do."

"But wouldn't that cut the water off for the entire block!"

"So?"

"Well, what happens if one of my thousand or so neighbors want water?"

"They can go down to the basement and switch on the mains," Strugurescu replied matter-of-factly.

"That would make my bathroom water come back on," I cried.

"Well, then you can go down to the basement and switch the mains off," Strugurescu said.

"It is hopeless talking to you."

"I drove the Traban over today. You wanted to try it. If you can drive it, we can go to the Music Conservatory today."

I was excited that finally I could learn to drive in Romania. After switching off the water for the thousand families, we went out into the street where I was introduced to a light pink Traban.

"Let me show you how to start this car," Strugurescu said, sliding in the passenger's seat. "You have to press this button to prime it. It has a 2-stroke engine"

"Like the lawnmower I once had," I murmured behind the wheel.

I pressed the button, turned the key, but nothing happened.

"It doesn't start," I said.

"You have to coax it to start. Be gentle with it - like with a girl."

I didn't know whether he was talking about the car or the girl.

After another minute or two of coaxing, the engine suddenly burst into life. Unfortunately, as the engine caught, a thick greasy plume of smoke shot out from underneath the steering column and splattered me in oil.

"What happened?" I choked. "Did the engine catch fire?"

Strugurescu bayed and guffawed like a donkey upon seeing my black face, neck, and shirt.

"That happens quite frequently. I have to mix oil with the gas. Sometimes it doesn't burn properly."

"You could have warned me."

"Keep your eyes on the road!" Strugurescu warned.

Gingerly, I steered the car down the street. I had not gone more than a hundred meters when a pack of stray dogs stormed out of a side street straight for the Traban. They looked like the same pack that had chased the pigs yesterday. They bounded, leaped, and snapped at the Traban.

I swerved to miss them and nearly crashed into a Mercedes parked by the side of the road.

"I hope we do not look like a big, pink pig to them!" I cried.

"They are color blind!" Strugurescu yelled back. "Be careful how you drive."

I swerved crazily down the street as the dogs continued hounding the Traban.

"No, they're not. They just cannot see red and green. They see pink very well."

"You just do not know how to drive this car!" Strugurescu shot back.

I took one turn around the block followed closely by the pack of neighborhood stray dogs. We arrived back at the front of the building where we had started from.

"You are right," I said, switching off the engine. "I cannot drive this car. We'll go to the Conservatory another day. How do we get out now?"

"The dogs look tired. Let's run fast into the building."

"You are right again. They do look tired."

We sprinted into the building. The dogs watched us uninterestedly as we exited. Their eyes were fixed on the pink Traban.

After switching on the mains, I cleaned up and made more coffee.

"Why are there so many stray dogs here in Romania?" I asked.

A relaxed Strugurescu sipped his coffee before replying. "To answer that question, you have to understand a little of our country's history. When Ceausescu razed private houses to the ground and began moving the population into these huge apartment blocks, many people had to give up their animals because the flats were just too small. So they abandoned their dogs in the streets. After a few years, the dog population multiplied."

"But these are not tame house dogs!" I exclaimed. "They seem to love to bite and kill. The ones I saw have open sores and fleas. They may even have rabies. Why don't the people here do something about the dogs before something bad happens? It would be tragic if the dogs attacked a child.'

"Oh, they do! Children and adults get attacked all the time!"

"And nobody does anything?" I asked incredulously.

"We did try to cull the dogs once," Strugurescu replied heatedly. "City Hall actively culled the stray dogs until Brigitte Bardot, a French activist, stepped in and persuaded some bureaucrat to halt the killings. Then other foreign animal rights activists, who never had their children mauled, got involved too. They suggested sterilizations! They forgot these are street dogs, not smiling dogs on veterinarian's tables waiting for somebody to sterilize them. There are too many decrepit places for dogs to hide in in this city. Furthermore, the dog catchers hired were poorly paid, illiterate, and easily bribed by the activists not to catch the dogs. Now City Hall is paralyzed – they do not know what to do anymore."

"You could put all the stray dogs in a shelter," I suggested.

"There are more than half a million stray dogs here!" Strugurescu balked. "Who's going to pay for taking care of half a million mangy stray dogs when people cannot even take care of their own families?"

"I don't know but something has to be done! Every time I go out, I have to run away from dogs."

"I think they like Chinese fast food," Strugurescu joked.

"That's not funny!" I remarked.

Years later in 2006, the unresolved stray dogs' problem almost caused an international incident. A Japanese financial consultant, Hajime Hori, had his femoral artery ripped out by stray dogs as he was entering his apartment block. He bled profusely and died almost immediately. Animal rights activists immediately hired a lawyer to protect the accused dog.

The accused dog, now named Boschito, and the other strays had their day in court. Strugurescu was proven wrong. The verdict was unanimous – stray dogs preferred sushi to Chinese!

13. Craters

A week later, I bought my first car. It was a brand new Romanian built gold colored, sport utility vehicle (SUV) by the name of Aro. It was roughly half the size of a normal SUV. The personnel from the factory delivered it to the front of the building where I lived. I called Strugurescu, who was still AWOL from the army and seemed to be enjoying it very much, and asked him whether he would like to go out for a drive.

He showed up in record time and examined the new vehicle with his tongue hanging out of his mouth. I swear he even salivated.

"This car is beautiful!" he exclaimed, stroking the paintwork.

"I need to get to know this city better," I said. "I'm willing to take you anywhere you want. But first I have to get to the Music Conservatory to put up an announcement."

"Great! I need to collect my salary from the army base. You can drive me there after the Conservatory. After that, you can drive me home and I will introduce you to my wife and son."

"Sure. That is no problem. I would love to meet your family."

We hopped into the car. I turned on the ignition and the engine jumped to life.

"Look!" I could not help saying. "No oil in my face."

Strugurescu smiled widely. He seemed to be in an excellent mood.

"You will have to guide me," I said. "I really have no idea where I am or how to get anywhere."

"Go straight down this road," Strugurescu said. "When you get to the market where you hid from the pigs and dogs, make a right. The Conservatory is in the city and the army base is just a little outside of the city. We will have a long drive."

We set off, but I had driven for no more than ten minutes, when I observed something disturbing.

"Wait!" I said. "Did you see that?"

"See what?" Strugurescu said.

"That car just disappeared. I saw it happen in the rear-view mirror."

"Cars don't just disappear," Strugurescu replied, his philosophical hat on.

"I swear to you that one did," I said. "Let me turn around and show you that I am not kidding you."

"You're the driver."

I did a fast U-turn and drove back quickly. As we approached the spot where I thought the car had vanished, I had to admit I was wrong in my original perception. One-half of the car had *not* disappeared.

"Look!" I said excitedly. "Somebody drove into a hole right in the middle of the street in broad daylight. I didn't even see it myself."

"Umm!" Strugurescu muttered back.

"How can you be so uninterested? Somebody's car just fell into a gaping hole! It could have been us. Look at the back of the car sticking up into the sky! The wheels are still spinning!"

"It happens all the time."

"What do you mean 'it happens all the time'?"

"If you drive here long enough, you'll get used to it too."

"I don't think I will ever get used to seeing the backside of a car sticking up in the air," I said, between clenched teeth.

We hurried out of our car. Other cars had stopped too, and soon there was a sizeable crowd gathered around the hole. People were chattering and jabbering like excited animals around a water hole.

"How could this happen?" I asked.

"Well, the driver drove into the hole," Strugurescu replied patiently.

"You don't seem to understand. There should not be a giant hole in the middle of a busy road. I don't see any barriers or lights to warn approaching drivers."

"There are holes everywhere in Romania. Actually, Romania is one big hole joined in parts by some roads. Having holes is normal but having roads…well, that is something you don't see everyday."

"Somebody must have dug this part of the road up. Maybe the gas or water company? Shouldn't they put up some warning signs around the hole?"

"Why would they do that?"

"To warn drivers," I said in exasperation. "Haven't you heard about barriers?"

"No point in putting up barriers," Strugurescu replied.

"I don't understand?" I said.

"Well, the gas or water company does not put up barriers anymore because the gypsies would steal them in the night. After the company loses a few sets, they don't bother anymore."

"The gypsies steal barriers?"

"Oh, yes. All the time."

"Why would they want to do that?"

"To sell them, of course!"

"Who would want to buy it from them?"

"For starters, the companies who supply the gas or water company with barriers. They buy it cheap from the gypsies and then resell it back to the gas or water company. They can do this their whole lives. What a racket."

"What about some alternate type of warning sign?"

"Sometimes, the people digging up the road will put a tree in the hole."

"A tree?"

"Yes, a tree or some big branches. That way, when drivers see a tree in their way, they will know that there is a hole there. Also, gypsies don't steal trees!"

"If I see a tree in the middle of the highway, I will think I have gone mad."

"Just to let you know, the other day a tractor fell into a hole and disappeared."

I stared at Strugurescu in consternation and was about to question him further when our discussion was interrupted by some shouts.

"I see the driver," a man shouted. "She is not hurt! Come and let's give the lady a helping hand."

I was all for helping so I moved in closer.

"The five of you there, climb and sit on the trunk," the man ordered. "Your combined weight will help lift up the front of the car. The rest of us will lift up the car from the sides."

"Is he joking?" I asked Strugurescu.

"Do you want to help or not?" Strugurescu shot back.

"I've never lifted up a car from a hole before."

"It's not so heavy. It's just a Dacia."

With muscles straining and backs creaking, the crowd got to work. The car leveled enough with the fresh weight on the trunk to allow the Dacia to be lifted up and pushed back on the road. The woman driver was flustered and thanked everybody through the rolled-down windows. Then without even getting out of her car, she started the engine and drove off down the street in a cloud of brown dust. She must have been in a hurry.

"Come on," Strugurescu said. "Don't stand there gawking. Let's go! I have to collect my salary before the office closes."

"Conservatory first," I remarked. "I just have to put up a notice."

"OK! Let's hope we do not see a truck in a hole. Sometimes gypsies steal large sections of road! Now that would take some work - to get a truck out!"

He saw my surprised face.

"You would never understand!" he remarked.

Strugurescu obtained his salary, I put up my notice at the Music Conservatory, and I also met his family that day. His wife was a svelte beauty with straight black hair but his son had inherited his chubby features and curly mop of hair. Strugurescu appeared to be a doting husband and father.

As I drove home that night, I wondered about Strugurescu's AWOL status, about the notice I had posted up at the music school, but most of all, I wondered about why the gypsies would want a huge section of a road.

14. Setting Up the Crusade

Now blessed with a car, I began scouting places in the city for a location which I could rent for a series of crusades. There was a huge building in the downtown area which I thought would be ideal, so I drove to the place early one morning.

I parked and tried to enter the building through the ornate gold front doors. But some guards at the doors redirected me to the kitchen entrance. I felt a little miffed that I had to use the delivery entrance. After some inquiries, I was led into the director's office which smelled musty.

"How much does it cost to rent this place for a series of meetings?" I asked.

The lugubrious director of the Great Hall peered at me down the length of his nose. He examined me the way a hungry lion would examine a freshly killed baby antelope that had dropped from the sky. With the scent of blood tingling in his thin nostrils, he leaned his lanky frame back in a scuffed up brown leather chair, lit up a cigarette, sucked on it greedily, and considered this unexpected windfall.

He did not answer my question immediately. Instead, he barked at his secretary, a pale, squat, grey-haired, stocky woman who resembled all Communist era propaganda posters. She was sitting behind a copper colored desk that looked in imminent danger of collapse. All manner of books, files, and clippings were higgledy-piggledy piled on one side of the desk causing the table to slant precariously.

"Quick! Get me our bookings book!" the director barked.

The secretary reached for the book and carefully extracted it from under a dangerously angled tower of books which somehow managed to stay upright. Then she shuffled over, hugging the three feet long tattered black book. She slammed the book down before her boss. A strong smell of mildew burst into the air. I couldn't be sure whether it came from the book or the secretary.

The director smiled at me through blackish-yellowish teeth. His gums were abnormally red - too much smoking and coffee combined with a complete lack of oral hygiene I presumed. He flipped through the pages of the book. Its yellowed pages were heavily marked with events dating back half a century. Pomp and past glory exuded from the faded black ink.

"The Great Hall is the pre-eminent concert hall in all of Romania," the director explained. "Here in this very place all major shows, political meetings, and concerts have taken place. Our history goes back to before you were born. The United Nations has held conferences here as well as The World Congress. Only recently, we rented out this place to Luciano Pavarotti as well as Michael Jackson."

He paused to let the name-dropping sink in. I could see the secretary at her desk furiously scribbling something but with her ears cocked towards us.

I smiled sheepishly. "I am no Michael Jackson or Pavarotti. But I would like to rent this hall Thursday night for a few months. I want to know whether the auditorium would be free and what the cost would be for each meeting."

The director picked up the book and turned some pages. After some time, he found the page he wanted. I noticed that it was blank. Thursday nights seemed to be a good choice.

"Normally we rent out this place only to famous people but we will make an exception this time. We have not received government allocated funds for a few months now and we need some money to pay our employees. As you can see, we seem to have Thursday nights free and are willing to give that slot to you provided you sign a contract with us for several months. That would ensure us of your seriousness to rent this venue. The rent money would help us through this difficult period."

I was elated. "So, what is the price for one night?"

The director stole a furtive glance at his secretary who was still busily scribbling on a pad steadfastly ignoring us.

He leaned forward. "I can give it to you for a round sum of US$1,000 per night. I am not interested in what you are doing as long as you pay us. We will sign the contract today upon payment of US$4,000 rent in advance – in our local currency, the Leu, of course."

I was taken aback at how fast everything was proceeding.

"I may have to think about it," I stammered. "I mean $1,000 per night is a lot of money." At that time, the price for an apartment was around US$5000.

"This sum is only valid today! If you come back tomorrow the price will be US$1,500 per night!"

I was caught and gulped. "When do you want the money?" The director smiled. He lit another cigarette. "Today by 4.00pm! Meanwhile, we will prepare the contract and finalize some other arrangements."

"What other arrangements?" I ventured.

"Oh! Things like ticketing and ushering.

We have to charge for those too."

"My meetings are for free. I do not require any tickets and seating is first-come first-served."

The director's melancholic eyebrows shot up. "You are not charging any entrance monies? Aren't you putting on some type of concert?"

"No, I am doing meetings and they are free of charge," I explained patiently.

"Are you mad? Nobody rents this place and opens it to the public for free! This is The Great Hall!"

"Well," I said. "Then this will be a first."

The director harrumphed like a horse with an apple stuck in its throat. "I hope that you will not open up my place to gypsies!"

"The meetings are for everybody!" I insisted. "Look! Do you want to rent out this place or not? I am willing to pay you a lot of money for it."

The director's lust for money battled with his passionate hatred for gypsies. I could almost smell the wheels in his head burning on overdrive. Money won out.

"I suppose it's not my business who you admit to your meetings. But if any gypsies show up, we reserve the right to refuse them entry. And if there are any damages to the building after the meetings, you will be responsible for them."

I breathed a sigh of relief. "Then it's settled. I will bring you a cashier's check by 4:00 pm."

The director's mouth fell open. The cigarette in his mouth fell onto the book. For a few seconds, there was a flurry of activity as he tried to extinguish the cigarette that was threatening to wipe out fifty years of recorded past grandeur. He succeeded thereby guaranteeing another fifty years of future appointments in the venerable black book. He turned back to me his voice tremulous with shock.

"We don't accept checks. Only cash!"

I sounded equally shocked. "Surely you don't expect me to carry that much cash, do you? The exchange rate is one dollar to 18,000 Romanian Lei. I can't walk around town with 72,000,000 Lei! At the very least, can you accept US dollars?"

"No, we cannot! All our business must be conducted in lei. That is the law. We can only accept Lei!"

"All 72,000,000?"

"Yes! All 72,000,000! Don't worry, we have counting machines here."

"I wasn't worried about that," I mumbled to myself.

The director stood up. His lugubrious look had vanished. He looked almost jovial. He reached out his hand and grabbed mine.

"Until 4:00 pm then. We will have the contract ready for your signature. It will be legal and all our terms will be on it.'

I shook his hand reluctantly. He rang and some guards rushed in to escort me out. They looked like the same guards that had refused me entry earlier. But this time, they led me out by the gold front doors. They even opened the doors for me as I left the place. I guess US$1,000 a night will open doors where none existed before.

15. On What It Feels Like To Be A Millionaire

I drove back home, dug out $4,000 from my second-hand Whirlpool washing machine where I had hidden it, and hurried to an exchange office. Walking with $4,000 in my pocket at a time when the average wage in Romania was less than US$100 per month, was nerve racking. All my previous experiences heightened my awareness of how vulnerable I was. But I reached the exchange office without incident.

The line for exchanging Lei was long, stinky, and fragrant all at the same time. Unwashed bodies of sweaty laborers stood shoulder to shoulder with richly perfumed ladies adorned with thick gold chains. The ladies stared at the laborers with suspicion. In turn, the laborers stared at me with suspicion. I tried to look at the white washed wall of the exchange office.

The clock ticked by slowly. 2:45 pm became 3:00 pm and then 3:15 pm. I realized I had only forty-five minutes till 4:00 pm! The Great Hall was near by but I was cutting it close. At last, at about 3:30 pm, I reached the counter.

"I would like to exchange $4,000," I said.

The woman at the counter looked at me in surprise. "US$4,000? All of it?"

"Yes," I replied.

The woman turned around to one of her colleagues and they spoke in hushed tones. After this mysterious conversation, she turned to face me again.

"We have Lei in notes of 5,000 only."

"Don't you have any bigger denominations?"

"No, only 5,000. Do you want to change the money or not?"

I took a quick glance at my watch – 3:32 pm! There would not be enough time to find another exchange office. It had to be done here or not at all.

"Yes, I want it," I replied, pushing the US dollars forward.

The woman counted out neatly bundled stacks of 5,000 Lei notes. Each bundle resembled the size of a brick. She started stacking them in front of me. As she neared 72,000,000, the stack in front of me had mushroomed into a mini pyramid.

I stared at the pyramid. "How am I going to carry this?"

"Don't you have a bag?" the woman asked incredulously. "You are exchanging $4000!"

"I…I was expecting that you would have larger denominations," I stammered.

"Everybody carries a bag with them." Her tone was accusatory.

"Do you have a sack or something that I could borrow?" I pleaded. "I will return it to you, I promise."

"No, we don't!" she scolded. "You should have brought a bag!"

"But I can't carry this pyramid!" I cried. "What am I supposed to do?"

"There is a trash can outside this office. Maybe you can find a plastic bag inside."

I looked at my watch. It showed 3:50 pm! I had no choice but to follow her suggestion and hope to find something – anything!

I rushed outside the exchange office to look for the trash can. Sure enough there was a rusty, green trash can attached to an old wooden pole. I dug into the trash, but to my dismay and frustration, did not find any discarded plastic bags. I was about to give up when I realized that the trash can itself was lined with a black, plastic trash bag. I could use that! I grabbed the whole trash bag, overturned the contents of it back into the green container, shook it a few times, and ran back into the exchange office. The whole thing took less than a minute.

"Put all the money inside here!" I gasped.

"Are you sure?" the woman gasped too - but more from the stink emanating from the trash bag.

Without waiting for her, I toppled the pyramid and swept the blocks into the bag. I ran out of the exchange office. My watch showed 3:55 pm.

16. The Payment

With 72,000,000 Lei in a stinking plastic trash bag, I ran the 400 meters to the glittering, gold doors of The Great Hall. I was gulping for air worse than a fish trying to scale Mount Everest by the time I reached the director's office. The clock on his wall showed 4:00 pm.

I emptied the sack, stacked the pyramid of cash on his desk, and prayed that he would not notice the stench. It gave a completely new meaning to stinkin' money. The director leaned back in his chair and motioned to the squat secretary, who magically produced two counting machines. She fed the money into the machines. As the bills were sucked in and blown out the other end, I prayed that the exchange house had given me the correct change. Fortunately, the total came out to 72,000,000.

"Bring out the book," the director ordered.

The squat secretary scurried back to her desk and brought out the venerated book again.

"Fill in every Thursday night that he wants!" the director barked. "And bring him some coffee."

A small cup of Turkish coffee materialized in front of my eyes as I chose a date about a month and a half away to begin the series of crusades. As I sipped the bitter tar, the director produced a contract.

"I have left the contract dates open-ended. But I will block off roughly one year for you! Come with me now and let me show you our concert hall."

As we exited the office, the director barked at his secretary.

"Put that money into the safe. We will change it tomorrow to US dollars! No point in keeping the money in Lei and have it depreciate further!"

I bit down hard on my tongue.

The director oozed friendliness as he took me by my arm and led me to the foyer of the Great Hall. My eyes bulged as I stared at the immense gilded lobby with twin grand marble staircases sweeping off at either side. It was majestic to the point of ostentatious. We climbed up the sweeping marble stairs to enter the concert hall itself. As we entered the hall, the lights came on and I stared at the 4,000 orange-gold seats facing a lofty stage that stretched the length of the magnificent hall.

I swallowed hard – 4,000 seats? What had I signed up for?

17. Telemescu, the Music Student

The Music Conservatory was the preeminent music school in Romania. I had placed a simple announcement there earlier. The announcement was an offer to students who would like to sing at a series of crusades.

There had only been one call and I was meeting that caller today.

My first sight of Telemescu was a perfectly round face. His round face shone like a wheel of cheese punctuated by two eyes and a huge smile. Not unlike the smiley face on stickers, I thought. We shook hands and settled down in a classroom at the school.

"It's after school hours," Telemescu said. "No one will disturb us here."

Outside the room, a cacophony of piano music and screeching immediately started

"Thanks for coming," I said. "I am trying to get a few students to sing some songs at an upcoming crusade. You will be paid a small sum of money for your effort."

"The money does not matter," Telemescu replied quickly. "I love God and I want to help. Where are you going to hold the crusade?"

"I have rented a big hall. What I need now are some good voices. If you help me it will give you immediate exposure.

This will help your career when you graduate. You can also include this in your resume. Maybe you have a few friends who might be interested as well?"

"Don't worry," Telemescu beamed brightly. "I have many friends here in the school. I will tell them about this crusade. They love God and would be glad to help too. By the way, when does this crusade start?"

I gave him the dates. "Those are starting dates. There might be more after that, I just don't know. If you can speak to your friends, I will rent a discotheque and all of you can practice there. I have bought all the music instruments necessary, so you can start rehearsals immediately."

"That is great. I will call my friends and let you know when we can meet."

We shook hands and parted. Strangely, the scratchy piano and the screeching stopped then too.

. . . .

Telemescu had eight of his friends with him the next time we met at the local discotheque. As promised, I had rented it temporarily for practice sessions. After I had been introduced to his friends, we sat down to translate and practice some Praise and Worship songs.

"We have never heard such beautiful songs before," a girl said. "In my church, we use chants."

"I'm glad you like it," I replied. "I bought it from Australia."

"The songs are unusual but very nice," another boy said.

"Can we come here and practice whenever we like?" Telemescu asked. "The crusades are not that far off."

"I will pay for all necessary hours," I replied.

"Where will you keep all of this music equipment?" Telemescu inquired further. "We need it for practice."

"I will arrange for them to be stored here. That way, we don't have to transport it every time we need it. There is a security guard here so the equipment will be safe."

"That sounds perfect."

As Telemescu and his friends practiced, I went in search of the guard who turned out to be a cantankerous old man. He was dressed in a blue Soviet styled uniform. I explained to him that I would be storing my music equipment in a small room by the side of the discotheque.

I pointed at the room. "Nobody enters that room. Do you understand?"

The guard scowled at me and nodded sullenly.

"You open that door only for me. I will be here twice a week for practice. Maybe more later on."

"I understood you the first time," the guard grumbled sourly. "I open the door for you only."

"Let me introduce you to some of the people whom I am working with."

He followed me into the discotheque and I introduced him to Telemescu and his friends from the Music Conservatory. He acknowledged Telemescu grudgingly and ignored the others.

"He's drunk," Telemescu whispered to me, after the guard left the room. "His face is extraordinary red and his eyes are extraordinary bright."

The other students rolled their eyes in agreement.

"We rehearse here twice a week," I told the students. "You have just a few songs to go through."

"That's not a problem," Telemescu said. "We might be students but we are professionals in music. Furthermore, we know each other's voices so we can coordinate the songs exactly the way you want them. Don't worry, we want to help you."

"If you say so," I replied.

Things were finally moving in the right direction.

18. Flying Coffins and Dracula's Castle

I invited Telemescu over to my place a fortnight later. His round cheese face shone transcendent. I offered him some crackers for breakfast which he devoured. It was weird watching cheese eating crackers.

"The rehearsals seem to be coming along fine," I said, in an encouraging tone. "I really like the way your voices sound together."

Telemescu needed no encouragement. "The songs are new but we know music so it is easy for us. As you may know, our Romanian church music is very different though."

"In what way?" I asked.

"We chant and sing verses from the Bible and we use no musical instruments. I like your way much better. Guitars, synthesizers, drums – I really like the instruments. But I am not sure how many people will to come to your crusade. People are very traditional here and may dislike your way. You really have to know more about the traditions of Romania to understand us better. How much of this beautiful country have you seen?"

"Not much," I replied.

"Have you been to Dracula's castle?" he asked. "It is a well known tourist place."

"I've heard of it. I would love to visit the castle. How far is it from here?"

"Well, if we start now we can be there by this afternoon!"

"You mean, today!"

"Yes, I visited the castle when I was a kid. I enjoyed it very much. I would like to go back there."

I made up my mind - we would go! It would be a nice break from the city and the upcoming crusades. I tanked up the Aro and we set off for Dracula's castle.

We were no more than two hours out of town, driving on the main Northwest-Southeast two lane highway through Romania, when I exclaimed loudly.

"Do you see what I'm seeing?"

"Drive faster!" Telemescu commanded. "Catch up with that Mercedes and you will be able to see it better."

"Are you crazy?" I blurted back. "That's a Mercedes you're talking about. I'm driving an Aro. I don't think I can catch it."

"This car can do it," Telemescu said confidently. "It is built in Romania for Romanian roads. Just push the pedal to the floor."

I stomped on the gas pedal and the little Aro jumped forward leaving some of its innards on the highway. Telemescu was right, we were catching up with the Mercedes.

"I think I lost some parts back there," I said, worriedly.

"That's OK," Telemescu said jubilantly. "You can buy those parts that fell off tomorrow. I know a good discount car parts shop. The main thing is to catch up with that Mercedes."

Easy for him to say, I thought silently. After all, he didn't have to pay for those parts.

"Is that a real coffin sticking out of the Mercedes trunk?" I asked.

"Of course it's real," Telemescu replied. "If you are able to get close enough, you can take a picture of it. Your friends back in America will love this."

"The driver may not appreciate us snapping a picture of his coffin. It may have the body of a loved one inside."

"Don't worry. It may be empty."

"If you say so."

Fifty feet, then thirty. We closed the distance fast. I could see the coffin clearly now. A solid oak casket with decorative carvings on it. With one hand on the wheel, I flipped out my camera with the other. We were less than twenty feet away when a ninety degree bend came out of nowhere. My heart stopped as the Aro screeched almost on two wheels around the bend following the Mercedes.

Before I could recover, I noticed that the driver of the Mercedes in front of me had stomped on his brakes and was fishtailing violently - first to the left and then to the right. I stomped on my brakes too.

As the Aro started to slide to the left and the Mercedes to the right, I saw through the triangular opening, directly in front of us, a two-level hand hewn wooden cart drawn by an emaciated horse. Pots and pans dangled and jangled by its side. The driver of the cart was a gypsy with a huge bristling horseshoe moustache. He was brandishing a whip. Several colorfully dressed family members were riding in the hay piled high on top the wooden contraption. I could see a few other heads poking out from the lower level as well.

Right then, the gypsies were staring in horror at the Mercedes barreling down upon them. At the last second, the Mercedes swung violently to the left narrowly avoiding crashing into the horse and cart - but the coffin in the trunk tore loose and sailed out onto the road. It hit the road hard and the top burst open. A dead body slid out and started rolling diagonally down the highway.

I stared in terror at the two halves of the coffin and the dead body that seemed to be heading straight towards us.

"Oh God!" Telemescu screamed, climbing up on his seat. He looked like he was going to poop on the chair.

I couldn't even shout. My eyes were transfixed on the coffin and body. I stomped on the accelerator viciously and at the same time, wrenched the steering wheel hard to the left. The car flew into the oncoming lane and then barreled up the shoulder of the road.

"Did you hit the body?" Telemescu cried.

"I didn't feel any bump," I said between gritted teeth. "I think we missed it."

"Yes, you did," Telemescu said, staring out of the rear window.

"I thought I had killed a corpse. Let me go back there and see whether the driver needs help."

"Not a good idea," Telemescu warned, still staring out back. "Keep on driving. The Mercedes driver and the gypsies are arguing now. I can see other drivers stopping and getting involved too."

"You don't think that we should at least get out and make sure that everybody is OK?"

"Of course not! Gypsies carry knifes and I don't want to be there when a fight breaks out! If they see you, they will surely attack you."

I had been through that before and did not want to go through it again.

"I see your point. Anyway the guy was dead before he hit the road. Short of trying to resurrect the body, there is nothing much that I can do."

"We have many more hours to go," Telemescu reminded me.

As I drove carefully down the highway, dark thoughts formed in my head. It was strange how we encountered the dead body in the coffin on our trip to Dracula's castle. I wondered whether vampires were waiting for us around the next bend in the road.

৯৽৽ৡ

19. A Discussion on Dracula

Dracula's Castle, also known as Bran castle, was situated north of the city of Curtea-de-Arges. While magnificent and appropriately situated on a steep hill, it was a disappointment for me. I looked in all the rooms of the castle and found no dark dungeons, creaking caskets, sharp stakes, beautiful vampires, lusty hunchbacks, nor the blood sucking Dracula I was led to expect from the movies. In its stead, were a multitude of stoic German tourists, period furniture, stoves, and a few chains hanging on a wall. Everything was so neat, tidy, and beautiful. It was such a letdown!

Telemescu and I decided to have an early dinner in the front of the castle and drive back later that night. We bought some food, found some rocks, and settled down. I was still wondering about that coffin in the Mercedes.

"Why would somebody carry a coffin in their car anyway?" I asked, between bites of a sandwich.

"He has to take the body home for the funeral," Telemescu replied. "That's how it's done here."

"But don't you use a funeral home or hearse or something like that?"

"There are no funeral homes here in this country. All the services are done in the living room of the deceased persons' house. People get the cadaver home any way they can. The coffin is usually strapped to the top, on racks and transported that way. That Mercedes had no racks, so it was stuffed in the trunk. People in the villages may use a wheelbarrow, a horse drawn cart like the gypsies we saw, or a tractor."

"I guess you have to do what you have to do," I said, imagining a stiff riding a wheelbarrow. "Tell me more about this place though. It doesn't look anything like what I saw in the movies back home."

"Dracula, vampires, and the wolf man were all created by you guys," Telemescu mouthed.

"Not by me," I said, defensively. "Hollywood did that. Maybe you can tell me the true story."

Telemescu moved his bottom to secure a more comfortable place on the rock. He popped open a can of Coke.

"I'm a Coca-Cola man."

I waited patiently for the caffeine to loosen his tongue.

After draining his can and settling further into the solid rock, he was finally ready to talk.

"You have to understand a little bit about this region's history before I can explain to you who Bram Stoker based his character of Dracula on. Let's go back about 500 to 600 years to the fifteenth century. At that time, Romania as you know it today did not exist. There was an area called Wallachia, roughly present-day southern Romania, which was sandwiched between two very powerful forces. To the north, there was the powerful Catholic, Austria-Hungarian empire. To the south, there was the Muslim Ottoman-Turkish empire. Each was bent on annihilating the other."

"I remember someone telling me about that," I said. "The Muslim Ottomans fought against the Christian Europeans."

"Yes, the fighting lasted a long time especially here in the Balkans. At about that time, King Sigismund of Hungary founded a secret fraternal order of knights, the Order of the Dragon, to defend his empire against the Ottoman Turks. Around 1431, a courageous man, Vlad, who had fought valiantly against the Turks was admitted to this Order. The Romanian word for dragon is 'drac'. So, Vlad became Vlad Dracul or Vlad the dragon, since he was now a knight of the Order of the Dragon.

"Now, Vlad wanted to rule the region of Wallachia. So, he seized it by killing a ruling cousin, who was a prince. Thereafter, he became the new prince of Wallachia, or prince Vlad II. There was an earlier prince Vlad I somewhere, I just don't remember all the details. Unfortunately, Vlad II now found himself caught between serving the Order of the Dragon which he had sworn allegiance to and the mighty Ottomans. Being a crafty politician, he gingerly played both sides to his advantage siding with whomever gave him the best opportunities.

"As Constantinople, today known as Istanbul, toppled, the Catholic Hungarians needed Vlad II to block the invading Muslim hordes bent on conquering all of Europe. He became very important to the Hungarians. But Vlad II wanted to appease the Ottomans too. He did this by sending two of his sons to become the Muslim king's slaves. One of those sons sent was Vlad III. Now, in Romanian the word 'fi-ule' means the 'son of'. Therefore Vlad III became Vlad Drac-ule or son of Vlad the dragon."

"So that's where the word Dracula came from," I said enthusiastically.

"Yes. Anyway, between playing both sides of Christendom and Islam, Vlad II was assassinated. Vlad III or Dracula, was then released by his Turkish master and became ruler of Wallachia. First, helped by the Turks and then the Hungarians he continued his father's precarious game of trying to appease both the Hungarian and the Turkish empires. It was while he was ruling Wallachia, from 1456-1462, that his reign of terror started."

"What reign of terror?" I asked.

"Vlad Dracula liked to use all kinds of torture and execution; nails in heads, scalping, cutting off limbs, noses, ears and breasts, blinding, strangulation, skinning, burning, roasting and boiling alive, exposure to wild animals, mutilation of sexual organs, and impalement."

I sorted through the macabre list in silence.

Telemescu, mistaking my silence for incomprehension, started to elaborate. "Some Ottoman envoys were visiting Dracula but they refused to take off their turbans. This was because of their religion. This angered Vlad and he ordered the turbans to be fixed permanently to the envoy heads with nails. As for Turkish prisoners, he would have their limbs torn off and their private parts displayed. Some prisoners would have the skin of their soles peeled off, then covered with salt. Goats were then brought in to lick their salted soles. Now, goats were used because it was believed that their tongue's rough papillae would cause maximum pain. The German merchants living in Wallachia at that time fared no better. Their villages were burnt to the ground and they were hacked to pieces like cabbages."

"And mutilation of sex organs?" I gasped.

"Vlad enforced a very strict moral code upon Wallachia. Adulterous wives, maidens who lost their virginity and unchaste widows had their sexual organs cut out or were impaled through their vaginas on red-hot stakes. He even cut off the breasts of some women and forced their lovers to eat them. He would roast little illegitimate children and coerce their own mothers to eat them."

I was beginning to feel sick. "Boiling alive?" I inquired.

"Vlad would have a big, copper cauldron filled with water. This cauldron would have a lid full of holes. People were then put into the cauldron, with their heads through these holes, and boiled alive. The people would cry and scream until they were cooked to death. Once, a condemned gypsy leader protested that death by fire was contrary to the law of his tribe. Nevertheless, Vlad ordered him to be boiled alive in the cauldron and then compelled the members of his tribe to eat his flesh."

"And burning?"

"That's a good one. It was the way Dracula eradicated poverty. There were many poor vagrants, beggars, and cripples throughout his land. So one day he invited all of them to his castle and led them into a great hall where he had prepared a magnificent feast for them. The guests ate and drank late into the night. It was then that Dracula made his appearance. He asked his guests whether they wanted to be free from cares and worries - to lack nothing forevermore. When the guests responded in the affirmative, Dracula had the hall boarded up and set afire. None of the poor vagrants, beggars, and cripples managed to escape. Hence, in one stroke, he eradicated poverty."

"Out of that list, which was his favorite?" I asked.

"Hands down, that would be impalement. Do you know that he was also known as Vlad Tepes or Vlad the Impaler? One of his first acts as ruler was to impale all the older noblemen while the younger ones were forced to build Castle Dracula which we just visited. He saw them all as traitors. Once, he had thirty thousand nobles from the city of Brasov impaled. Then to better enjoy this sight, Dracula commanded that his table be set up amongst this forest of impaled corpses. While dining, he noticed one of his men holding his nose as if to alleviate the stench of rotting bodies and bowels. Dracula immediately ordered this sensitive man impaled on a stake higher than all the rest. This was done so that he might be above the stench. Dracula loved to walk among this forest of impaled bodies and exclaim about their exquisite beauty!"

"It sounds ghastly," I said weakly.

"Death by impalement was slow and painful," Telemescu agreed. "Victims sometimes endured for days before they died. One impalement method had the victim's legs forced apart by opposing horses tied to each leg. Then a sharpened stake was gradually forced into the body. The end of this stake was usually oiled and great care was taken that it was not too sharp - so that the entrails of the victims would not be pierced immediately by a fatal wound. Normally the stake would be inserted into the body through the anus or vagina and then hoisted upright. Thus, the victim was slowly impaled by the force of his or her own weight and gravity. Victims could also be impaled through other bodily orifices or through the abdomen or chest. Sometimes the victim would be impaled upside down. Oftentimes, the height of the stake would indicate the rank of the victim. Other times, Vlad

Dracula would arrange the stakes in geometric patterns like concentric circles. The decaying corpses, beautifully arranged, would be left up for months. An invading Turkish army once turned back in fright when it encountered tens of thousands of rotting impaled Turkish corpses. However, Vlad Dracula was finally killed by the Turks - he was decapitated and his head was sent to Istanbul where the Muslim king in turn displayed it on a stake for all to see. The frightened populace needed proof that Dracula had indeed died!"

"I don't blame them," I said. "He seemed to be much worse than the Hollywood version of Dracula."

"To you maybe but not to us," Telemescu replied. "We see him as a hero – a just prince who defended his people from the marauding Turks, Austria-Hungarians, and parasitical German merchants. He was a champion for the common man against the tyrannical landowners and capricious nobles of his time. Also, he was successful in eliminating crime, poverty, and immoral behavior in the region."

"But he impaled or burnt everybody to achieve that! You can eliminate almost anything if you kill everybody."

"That was Vlad's method," Telemescu said. "And Hollywood stole the idea of the stake through the heart from him. He should be paid royalties posthumously!"

I looked at the castle towering above me with a new set of eyes. I had been too quick to equate its present tidiness and touristy ambiance to tameness and 'boring-ness'. The history lesson I had just learned from Telemescu changed all that.

20. Corrupt Traffic Police

"Car registration papers and driving license!" the policeman snapped.

I peered at him through the darkness. We were snaking through the Carpathian Mountains on our way back home, when signaled to pull over. It was a dark, moonless night, made darker by the stories that Telemescu had told me at Dracula's castle.

"Here you are," I said, handing over the papers. "What did I do wrong?"

The policeman took my papers and shone his flashlight on them. His eyes lit up when he saw my New York state license. "You drove with your highlights on. It could blind the drivers coming from the opposite direction!"

"But there were no cars coming from the other side!" I protested.

"Yes, there were."

Then they must be ghost cars, I thought. I wondered whether he could see dead people too.

"I didn't see any!"

The policeman brushed off my objections. "Give me your passport."

I handed him my passport.

"Wait here!" he commanded.

"I'll wait! I can't go anywhere without my papers anyway!"

Telemescu could not contain himself anymore. "Do you know why he stopped you?"

"He mentioned that I was driving with my highlights on. I didn't see any cars approaching from the other direction, did you?"

"Of course there were no cars. He's giving you a hard time because you are a foreigner!"

"Why would he do that?"

"Because he wants money from you. Otherwise, he will take away your papers."

I stared at Telemescu. "No way! This is all just a mistake and will be resolved quickly."

"Yes way! Just wait and see!"

We waited and waited. I could see the policeman in his patrol car talking to his colleague. They were laughing and talking, making no sign of acknowledgment that we were waiting for them.

After ten minutes of fidgeting and second-guessing myself, I had enough.

"I'm going over there to talk to them!" I said.

"Do you want me to come along?" Telemescu replied sweetly.

"No, you stay here!"

I walked over to the patrol car. The laughter and conversation died down.

"We are still waiting over there," I began. "I was wondering…"

The policeman interrupted me. "You have broken the law. We are going to keep your car papers, license, and passport."

I was stunned. "You can't do that!"

"Oh yes, we can," he snarled at me. Then in the very next second, his countenance transformed into a benevolent, paternalistic visage. His tone dropped down several octaves.

"But we can resolve this! Give us fifty dollars and you can be on your way."

I nearly fell over in surprise.

The policeman continued smiling ear to ear. It hurt my face to see him smiling so broadly.

"We will give you all your papers back. Just be careful how you drive the next time."

"I didn't do anything wrong," I said. "And even if I did, why don't you just give me a fine?"

"We can give you a fine, but we still have to keep all your papers! Why would you want to pay a fine instead of solving this problem amicably between us? Furthermore the fine is much higher than fifty dollars!"

Suddenly, Telemescu materialized by my side.

"I thought I told you to stay in the car!" I said.

Telemescu brushed me aside and started a conversation with the policemen. There was an inordinate amount of nodding.

In the end, Telemescu turned around to face me.

"Give them the fifty dollars! That's the only way."

I couldn't believe my ears but fished out fifty dollars from my pocket. I walked back to my car in a huff, leaving Telemescu to seal the deal. He came back with all my papers.

After driving for a few minutes in silence, I could not contain myself any longer.

"That was highway robbery and extortion!" I exclaimed. "And you went with it!"

"Yes, I went with it to save you. They told me that they would have fined you a few hundred dollars if you had not paid up. They would also have kept all your papers and then accidentally, lose them somewhere afterwards. Then you would have no passport, no driving license, and no car papers. Furthermore, you will have to leave your car and trek through the mountains to the nearest town. There are plenty of hungry wolves in these wild mountains. What is fifty dollars compared to that?"

I mulled over this new information.

"Thank-you," I said to Telemescu.

"You are welcome," he replied, beaming like a saint.

I felt like I was driving home with the moon by my side. For Telemescu beamed rounder and brighter than the non-existent moon in the sky.

21. How to Promote a Crusade

The hall for the crusade had been rented. The students had been recruited from the conservatory. The next step was to advertise the series of crusades. Dutifully, following my visit to Dracula's castle, I drove to the printers and collected my order for 30,000 flyers. My heart jumped for joy as I looked through the colorful invitations. The flyers were to be my publicity tool for the upcoming crusades. They were packed and ready to go.

I didn't waste any time. The flyers were to be distributed immediately. I chose the city center as the point of distribution. Thousands of people passed through the location I had selected. In distributing flyers, just as in house selection, it was always location, location, and location.

"Hello!" I smiled at a passerby. "I have something for you." I was to repeat this sentence thousands of times in the next few days.

"Are you opening a Chinese restaurant?" she asked.

"No, it's for a crusade.'

A blank look appeared on her face. "Oh! I'm not interested. What's a crusade?"

"Well, there will be some songs and there will be a message after that."

Her eyes lit up. "Something like a rock concert?"

"Not exactly," I said, "But it will be far more interesting."

"Not interested!"

Other answers were even more interesting.

"We are all Christians here in this country," a man told me. "We were born as Christians. Why do we need a crusade?"

"Do you know Jesus Christ personally?" I asked.

"Who cares? He died thousands of years ago. He no longer helps us because he's dead. We have many churches here that help us."

"That's not the same," I countered.

"Sorry! Not interested in an old dead man! Our church will save us."

An old homeless man shuffled by.

"Are you handing out coupons for free food?" the old man asked. He looked like he had not eaten for a long time.

"Yes! Spiritual food," I replied.

"Eh! What did you say? If you are not giving out free food, get out of my way! You're just wasting my time."

Then out of nowhere, a young boy rushed up to me. I handed him a flyer. He read through it and smiled. I thought I had my first sympathizer.

"Come for the crusade," I cajoled him. "You will like it."

"Can I ask you something?" he said.

"Of course!" I replied, ready to tell him more about Jesus.

He turned around, dropped his pants, and pulled down his underwear.

"Can you read these Chinese characters?" he asked. "I don't know what they mean."

I stared at his flat white butt. It had Chinese lettering tattooed on it.

"I don't read Chinese," I said apologetically.

"Oh!" he said sadly. "Thanks for looking!"

He hitched up his pants and walked off, throwing the flyer onto the ground.

Next , a woman came up to me and started crying. "Priest! Priest!" she cried.

I handed her a flyer. She folded it carefully and dropped it between her watermelon size breasts still crying a river. She shot off a string of words, squeezed my face in her hands, and then departed. I didn't know what to make of that.

For the most part, people on the street just ignored my outstretched hands. Some ran away as fast as they could, while others put the flyers in their pockets. I just prayed that they would not discard the flyer in the next trash basket down the street. Fortunately for me, there were very few trash baskets in Romania at that time.

I did this all day, skipping lunch and dinner, and managed to give away about 3,000 flyers. When night came, I called it a day and went back home.

22. How Not to Promote a Crusade

I distributed flyers for several days before something unexpected happened. A call came through one evening.

"What do you think you are doing?" a hysterical voice yelled.

I didn't recognize the voice.

"Come in tomorrow morning at 8:00 am!" the voice screamed. "In my office at the Great Hall!"

It dawned on me then that the screaming voice belonged to the director of the Great Hall. I endured a sleepless night. Was the money I had given to him not good? Was it counterfeit? Many days had passed by. Why did he call now?

I was in the director's office by 7:55 am the next morning. The moment the director caught sight of me, he burst out frenetically.

"Stop what you are doing immediately!" he shouted, throwing one of my flyers in my face. His secretary disappeared under the untidy files that still littered her desk.

"What's wrong?" I asked puzzled. "What did I do?"

"I hear you are distributing thousands of these flyers in the center of the city!" he accused.

"Yes I am!" I said, surprised that was the reason he had called me in so urgently.

"Stop that! You cannot hand out any more flyers!"

"Why not?" I asked, genuinely surprised. "I am trying to let the public know I am holding crusades here. How else are they to know?"

"I don't know and I don't care!" the director shouted in a frenzy. "But you must stop the flyers. I can't have you distribute religious flyers in the center of the city with my Great Hall written on it! You are a cult and you are proselytizing.'

"How is anybody going to know where the crusades are unless I mention the place?"

The director twitched convulsively, as though in great pain. "You cannot name this place for a crusade! I cannot be involved in a crusade!"

"We signed a contract," I reminded him. "I paid you the money!"

He held his head in his hands. His eyes revealed his terror of something or someone.

"Look!" he pleaded. "Just don't distribute any more flyers in the city center and I will let you have some crusades here. Let me speak to some people first."

"I still don't know what you are talking about," I said. "I've already paid you!"

I left him, his head in his hands.

֎

23. How to Kill a Crusade

A million thoughts went through my mind that day. Why was he so angry? What had the director meant when he ordered me to stop distributing flyers? I figured I still had 21,000 plus flyers undistributed! How and where had he gotten his hands on one of my flyers? Surely I would have remembered if I had passed one to him on the streets. It was all too confusing.

I made up my mind. I had paid a lot of money for the hall, and I was not going to let the director frighten me. I had to advertise the crusades. Otherwise, nobody would come for them and all the money would be wasted. In the Bible, we are called to be stewards or managers of what God has given to us. It calls us to be good stewards, not bad ones. So, I was not going to waste the resources given to me.

The director had insisted that I stop distributing the flyers in the city center. So I figured that I would go underground – literally. The underground subway system carried a few hundred thousand people every day. I would hand out the flyers there instead. I chose the busiest underground subway hub, which was three floors down, and positioned myself on the exit stairs. That way, all passengers exiting the station had to pass by my extended hands. I must have cleared 6,000 flyers that day before I went back home.

Then déjà vu!

The director called again and ordered me to come in to see him the next morning. I was there punctually.

"Why did you disregard my order to stop distributing flyers?" the director thundered. "I told you to stop! Yet you are still distributing!"

"How do you know that?" I blurted, a little perplexed.

"Fool! I have people following you! We know where you are at all times! You were in the subway interchange handing out those flyers. You thought we will not know if you go underground. I'm going to cancel your contract and you can have your money back!"

I was dumbfounded.

"How much did you pay us? I can have it all back to you by today."

I had laughed when Black Bear had told me about Mrs. Urdescu and the communist era spies. It had seemed like a joke, almost unreal, till now. My blood froze as I realized that somebody was tracking my every step. They knew where I was – even though I was three floors under the earth! All the stories I had heard about communist intelligence-gathering spies came back to taunt me now. If there was a good time to give up, this was it.

Then a holy courage rose up in me. "If you cancel the contract, I will sue you!"

The director could not believe his ears. "You will not win!"

"Maybe not, but you will probably lose your job!"

The director did not relish that prospect. "Look! There's no need to sue. I will honor two of your crusades. That is all I can do. But you must stop passing out those flyers."

I was about to argue further for my rights when a revelation hit me. The director was being pressured from somebody else! It was probably from some powerful religious leaders' intent on stopping the crusade. I remembered reading about other cancelled crusades planned in stadiums and led by world renowned evangelists. I was a nobody and I was not going to win this fight. The director was clearly nervous and upset. It was not my intention to make him lose his job and I actually felt sorry for him.

"I accept," I said. "Two crusades it is then."

With more than half the flyers left undistributed, the first crusade still managed to attract approximately 1600 people. It was similar for the next crusade. There were many salvations but there was no support for the people after that. There was no discipling for I had no place to disciple anyone. I felt clearly, in my spirit, that I had not achieved what God had called me to do. The realization that I was tracked by spies left me deflated. I had to take a short break to clear my muddled head.

24. Corrupt Border Guards

He was young and without fear or shame. I eyed him carefully. No more than twenty-three, he had insolence written all over him. I felt that if I needed to, I could take him down. But he had a gun by his side and he was wearing an official uniform of the border police. If I touched him, I knew that many other young, fearless, shameless, and insolent border policemen, with guns, would materialize and lock me up for good. I wasn't ready to be locked up.

The crusades had ended and I was taking a break visiting a neighboring country. I had driven to the Romanian border cheerfully.

"Give me US$100!" the border police commanded.

"Why should I give you $100?" I asked, mystified.

"Because you are a foreigner and you have money," he replied.

I appreciated his directness. "But what did I do? I'm just leaving the country for one day and will be back the following day."

"You give me $100 or we will not let you pass."

From behind him, three other insolent border guards appeared as if out of thin air. They stared at me with impunity.

Now, courage is not the absence of fear but the will to continue on despite the fear!

"I don't have any money to give to you!" I challenged.

He could not believe his ears. I knew for a fact, that most foreigners pay when commanded. He motioned to his three colleagues, who strolled over nonchalantly. They gazed at me like owls at a noisy mouse.

"Give us the money!" they warned. "Don't play with us."

"I don't have any money!" I protested.

The owls turned to parrots.

"Give us the money!" they repeated. "Give us the money!"

"Don't you get it? I am not giving you any money!"

"Give me your passport and car papers!" the first guard snarled.

Here we go again, I thought, as I handed him the passport and papers. The episode with the traffic police up in the Carpathian Mountains was still fresh in my mind.

Behind me, the line to cross the border grew. Cars began honking furiously. The guards got mad and started bellowing at the other drivers. The honking stopped. I was praying for the guards to let me go.

"Are you carrying any drugs or contraband cigarettes?" another guard asked.

"No, I'm not! You can search the car all you want."

That was the wrong thing to say. Immediately, the guard jumped on the opportunity.

"If you do not give us the money, we will search your car completely."

"Fine! Why don't you do that? I have nothing to hide."

They directed me to park in an adjacent lane and proceeded to leisurely and methodically tear the car apart. The dashboard and the seats were stripped out first. I stood by watching.

"Are you Christians?" I asked.

No answer. Then one of them replied. "I go to church once a year. Why?"

"I'm a pastor and an evangelist. Let me tell you about Jesus Christ. I have a Bible here in my car."

After five minutes, three of the border guards stood up, dropped their tools, and walked off, leaving the first guard alone. He was a captive audience and I worked on him. He sweated profusely trying not to answer any of my questions.

As he started dismantling the driver's door, I shared with him from Luke. When he got to the passenger's side door, I got to John. After two hours, some of his colleagues came back to help him and I started sharing with them again. I was reliving Paul's experience when he was chained to the guards in prison and he shared the Word of God with them.

"Do you want to go for a beer?" one of the guards said finally. "Your throat must be dry."

"No," I replied. "I want to be here. Now, let me tell you about grace."

The guards groaned. I was sure they wanted me to shut up but I was beginning to enjoy myself. I wrote down my address and invited them to come and visit me. They passed the piece of paper amongst themselves, not knowing what to do with it. I started sharing with them about faith, as they took the wheels off and peered under the chassis and engine. It was a great six hours, in which the border guards found nothing but God!

When they finally finished and had assembled the parts back, they couldn't wait to wave me through the border.

"I'm coming back tomorrow," I said cheerily, as I drove through. "I'm going to stop and talk to all of you some more."

The guards turned their backs on me with unanimity and walked off dejectedly. They were nowhere to be found when I drove back into the country the next day.

25. Children of the Sewers

As for Strugurescu, the army finally found him and called him in. He had a week to report to his superiors. But he didn't seem overly worried about it.

"I don't really want to go back, but I need the money," he said. "Can we go out and do something together before I go back to my boring job? I cannot understand why we need to have an army because NATO and American forces are here already. I hear that our neighbors, the Hungarian army, are deployed in the plains cutting grass! They do not have anything to do either. I hope we do not have to cut grass."

"It's a great thing to be defending your country," I replied.

"Defend against who?" Strugurescu asked in great astonishment. "Who would want to come here? Everybody here is doing their best to leave! The last man to leave can turn out the lights!"

I purposefully switched topics. "Listen! I want to go around and see whether I can find other halls to rent for crusade purposes. You may not know this but I was kicked out of the Great Hall."

Strugurescu shook his head. "I didn't know that, but once you get kicked out of one venue, you will be blacklisted! The directors all know one another and they pass information along to each other."

"That's ok; I just want to make sure this particular door is closed before moving on."

"What door?" Strugurescu asked looking around.

"Never mind," I said. "Let's get to the city and walk around a bit. I have a few places I would like to check out."

After visiting the few places on my list Strugurescu was proved correct again. Nobody would rent their facility for a crusade! This was not going well at all.

I shook my head despondently. "Let's get back. It's already getting dark."

As we walked back to the car, I tripped and nearly fell headlong into an open manhole.

"Where is the cover?" I asked, astounded, picking myself up. "I mean, anybody can fall into one of these open holes, especially when there are no street lights."

"You are right," Strugurescu replied. "Many people have fallen into manholes. My father fell into one of these holes about thirty years ago and he still walks with a limp to this day."

I stopped and stared at Strugurescu. "Are you serious?"

"Of course! I would not make up such a story."

"But didn't your father sue the city? Or somebody? In America, you can sue anybody!"

"Over there, yes, but not here. The courts are corrupt and you can always bribe judges to look the other way. We did not have any money so there was no point in suing anybody."

"But your father did not go to see a lawyer at all?"

"The lawyers are even worse. They want a lot of money up front and then may pack up shop and disappear."

"I don't believe that!" I said. "Lawyers do not operate like that."

"Believe what you want but you have a lot to learn about this culture. By the way, the reason as to why there are no manhole covers is that the gypsies have stolen all of them."

"Whatever for?" I asked.

"To sell, of course! There are many junkyards here that will buy scrap metal from the gypsies."

"But don't the scrapyards know that the metal is stolen? I mean, a manhole cover is a manhole cover. You cannot disguise it as an old pipe."

"They know, but they don't care. After all, they pay just a few cents for a few pounds of scrap metal. So the gypsies steal all the manhole covers they find. On top of that, they steal all the metal street signs and fire hydrants, too. Some of them even steal rail tracks and the copper wires used by the trains for signaling. I once heard that in Ukraine, the gypsies stole an entire train and a bridge! Anything that is bolted down can be unbolted. The metal roofs of churches go the same way. It is easy money for both the gypsies and the junkyard owners. Some of these junkyard owners are millionaires and live in castles. Many times, these junkyard owners are gypsies themselves."

I had a momentary vision of cars driving off into bucolic pastures for lack of signs as well as trains flying off tracks and bridges that were no longer there and disappearing into black holes and other portals. As I was pondering the improbability of it all, another unexpected event occurred!

A head bobbed out at my feet! I nearly fell over in surprise. It took me a few seconds to realize that a child had just materialized out of the street. I took a few steps back as the body attached to the head climbed out of the manhole.

She could not have been more than ten years old with unkempt long brown hair bundled behind her head. Her clothes were soiled and looked like a cross between a pair of pajamas and something that a hip-hop star would wear. She was covered with dirt from the top of her head down to her bare feet. She wore the biggest smile I had ever seen and her eyes were as big and as deep as walnuts. I noticed that one of her arms was broken at the elbow with the bone sticking out at an awkward angle. But she still had one good hand which was extended towards me.

"5,000 Lei," she begged. "5,000 Lei please!'

"Go away and leave us alone!" Strugurescu hissed.

The little girl was unfazed. "5,000 Lei," she insisted.

"She must have heard us talking," I said. "But what was she doing underground?"

"Oh! Don't you know that they live there? There are several hundred, maybe a few thousand, children who live in the sewers."

"Why do they live in the sewers?" I asked in astonishment.

Strugurescu looked back at me in equal astonishment. He must have thought I was slow or something. He replied like he was explaining to a 5-year-old boy. "Because there are hot water pipes down there. That is how they keep warm at night."

"Ooh!" I said, registering comprehension. "Let me give her the 5,000 Lei. That's only about a quarter, isn't it?"

"You cannot help her that way," Strugurescu said.

"What do you mean?"

"What I mean is that whatever you give to her will be confiscated by her pimp."

"She's got a pimp?"

"Yes! They have a pimp who controls them and takes away all their money. Furthermore, if you take out your wallet in plain sight, she may be tempted to run away with it."

"Please, just 5,000 Lei!" the gypsy girl pleaded loudly.

"Ask her what happened to her hand," I said. "Did she fall down climbing in and out of that sewer?"

Strugurescu turned to the girl and fired off some questions rapidly. The girl replied unabashedly.

"What did she say?" I asked impatiently.

"No, she did not fall," Strugurescu replied.

"Then how did she break her arm?"

"She said her father broke her arm."

I was stunned. "Her father broke her arm? But why would he do a thing like that?"

The little girl mumbled something to Strugurescu.

Strugurescu translated for me. "Her father broke her arm so she would be able to earn more money begging. People would give her more money if she was maimed. If she's perfectly healthy, people may not have any pity on her. But after her father broke her arm, she was afraid and ran away from home. Now she lives in the sewers. At least she has friends here, a pimp who protects her, and she does not need to be afraid of her father anymore."

"Why doesn't she go for help somewhere?"

"Who would want her?" Strugurescu asked. "There are thousands like her here. Also, she would not want to be in a home. She likes it on the streets where she enjoys complete freedom and can beg for a living. To appear even more pitiable, she may borrow a baby from her friends and drug it, before begging."

"Drug the baby? Why?"

"So it doesn't cry and interrupt the begging!"

"5,000 Lei," she whined, tugging at my pants.

I looked at her. "Why would a 10-year-old want complete freedom? Doesn't she want somebody to take care of her? I mean she can't be happy with fleas in her hair and sores all over her legs."

Strugurescu laughed. "Stop thinking like an American. Be more Romanian. Listen to me, she does NOT want somebody to take care of her. Here she can smoke, sniff glue and metal polish, have sex, steal, beg, and be free as the wind. In a home she would have to go to school, dress up and bathe. Why would she want that? Fleas and sores are nothing compared to rules and regulations. Her pimp gives her complete freedom as long as she gives him some money."

I was taken aback. "I just thought everybody wanted a nice home."

"Not them. They would die under the rules."

"So how do I help them?" I insisted.

"You cannot!" Strugurescu said. "They are gypsies and you cannot change a gypsy!"

"God can change anybody," I said.

"Hmmm!" Strugurescu sounded unconvinced.

"5,000 Lei," the gypsy girl sniveled. "5,000 Lei."

"What am I suppose to do?" I asked.

Strugurescu shook his head. "Do whatever you want."

I dug into my pockets and found 10,000 Lei or roughly 55 US cents.

"Here you are," I said, pressing the coins into the little girl's palms.

The impossibly wide smile on her face widened even more. I smiled back. The next second, much to my amazement, another ten gypsy girls materialized from out of nowhere, surrounded me, and began chanting, "5,000 Lei! 5,000 Lei!"

Strugurescu fled from the scene, his thin legs knocking and flying over the pavement.

I grabbed the remaining loose change from my pocket, emptied it into the hands reaching out for me and fled down the street in pursuit of Strugurescu.

My mind was preoccupied on the drive back.

"I cannot get that maimed little girl out of my mind. I mean, there's got to be orphanages or homes who would take her in."

"They wouldn't want to be in an orphanage!" Strugurescu said in a disgusted tone.

"Why?" I inquired. "Is it that bad? Maybe we can go and visit one tomorrow."

"If you really want to," Strugurescu said, gloomily.

"Yes, let's do that tomorrow."

26. Food for Rats: A Visit to a State Orphanage

"Quick! Give me fifty dollars!" Strugurescu whispered to me.

"Why?" I said, dropping my voice. "Why do you need the money?"

I wondered why I was whispering.

"We have to pay the nurse to allow us to enter!" Strugurescu replied, in a secretive tone.

"I don't like to bribe people," I breathed back darkly.

"I know you don't," Strugurescu said. "Just give me the money and I will bribe the nurse."

"There's more than one nurse," I argued. "Do we have to bribe all of them?" I saw at least three more nurses huddled together, staring at us furtively from the shadows of the entrance to the state orphanage.

"Don't worry. Fifty is enough. They will share the money among themselves."

"Are you sure of this? This is not illegal, is it?"

Strugurescu snickered. His thin body shook with mirth as his mind struggled to grasp the ridiculous nature of my question.

"Everybody bribes in this country. Corruption affects seven out of every five people here! That is how we survive. Just give me the money."

"Don't you mean five out of every seven?"

"No, I mean what I said!"

Reluctantly, I pulled out a fifty-dollar bill from my wallet.

"Don't show everyone the money," Strugurescu intimated furiously. "Cover it with something." He palmed the bill with ease with his long thin fingers.

"But you just told me that everybody takes money here."

"Yes, I did. But we pretend it doesn't happen." He ambled languidly over to the head nurse.

The head nurse was an enormous woman, her girth about equal to her height, and with purplish-blue hair styled in big curls. The sourness of her face transformed as she, in turn, palmed the bill with practiced ease. A beatified smile spread across her face as she immediately beckoned us to follow her into the institution.

I followed the coattails of Strugurescu, who in turn followed the starchy crispness of the head nurse's white skirt. She crackled with pride and haughtiness as she smuggled us in. Behind us, the other mousy nurses quickly barred the front entrance. I wondered how much their share of the loot would be.

We did not speak as we were whisked along marbled corridors yellowed with neglect and disrepair. It was cold and clammy even though the sun shone brightly into the passages that we traversed through. It was also eerily quiet - not a child peeped through the tall imposing doorways. The ornate carvings on the doors, now in disrepair, highlighted the paint peeling off them in long strips. We walked up and down nameless stairs. Finally, it was just down until we arrived at a huge metal door. The head nurse mumbled something to Strugurescu before fumbling at the keyhole and swinging the door open.

"What did she say?" I asked.

"No pictures," Strugurescu translated. "They do not want to get into trouble."

I wondered about this cryptic remark before following him into the room.

A blanket stench of urine and moldy sweat hit me. The room was small, dark, dank, and pock-marked by sheaths of mold clinging to the walls. It resembled my bathroom. I hardly had time to adjust my eyes to the darkness of the dungeon when Strugurescu shouted.

"Whoa! There's a rat over there eating a child!" He started swearing as his hands pointed shakily to my left. I had never seen Strugurescu that way before. He looked like he had swine fever - his emaciated head shining with sweat and his whole body trembling like the last leaf on a tree in an autumn gale.

I looked to where he was pointing and what I saw almost made me swear too. In a corner of the dark room, a rat was eating a child!

The next moment I was bowled over by the gargantuan head nurse as she rushed towards the rat. I never thought a woman that size could move so fast. With the blurring speed of an express train, she reached the rat and kicked at it with her huge tree trunk leg limbs. The rat scurried away easily and crawled into a hole in the wall.

At the same time, the child now freed from the rat, started crawling towards a rusty metal bed. Once on the bed, the child clung to the metal bars that surrounded the bed on three sides and rocked himself back and forth violently. His head began to bang on the bars in a staccato rhythm. Blood dripped from his leg where the rat had chewed on him. I noticed that the metal bars on the fourth side of the bed had fallen down onto the floor. That must have been how he had slipped out.

In that same bed, I saw another three children. Two of them, quite small, were lying comatose on the bed. The other one, his head and face grossly enlarged by hydrocephalus, stared blindly upwards. They all seemed to have their sleeves tied up to prevent their little fingers from feeling anything.

In the next bed, another four children turned lifeless eyes to look at me. That was all they could do as their little bodies were tightly bound up with bed sheets as in a cocoon. I couldn't see their hands or feet at all. Many of them had vomit dribbling out of their mouths which coagulated on the yellowed sheets already stained by urine and excrement. Hanging on the bars of the bed were two feeding bottles roughly tied with some string. One child started sucking on this contraption with a gurgling noise that reminded me of an animal sucking on a water bottle. None of the children could have been older than five or six years old. All of them seemed visually impaired from the perpetual darkness of the dungeon. I stared rudely, too horrified to speak.

The head nurse moved to the first bed to right the fallen metal bars. Suddenly, from the back of the room where there were more beds cramped with misery, a boy broke free from the wretchedness and rushed towards us with his arms open wide. He had dark curly hair and the widest angelic smile on his lips as his short legs propelled the small body forward.

I squatted down to receive the child's embrace.

The child never made it. The head nurse stuck out her tree trunk leg and the child ran into it full tilt. He bounced a few inches backwards, rolled, and fell face down on the murky floor. He did not cry but picked himself up just as the nurse swung her arm and smote the boy on the back of his head with a resounding thud. The child fell down again, but still did not cry.

"What's wrong?" I asked shocked at the unprovoked beating.

"You cannot touch the children," Strugurescu translated.

"Why not?" I countered. "It seems to me that nobody has touched or held these children for years."

"The nurse does not want you to hold them because the children might expect somebody to hold them after you leave. The nurses are not paid to hold these handicapped children. Furthermore, she says that their hair is full of fleas and their skin full of cantankerous sores. She is very surprised that you would want to hold such dirty, smelly creatures."

At that moment the nurse broke out into a long stream of expletives.

"What did she say?" I asked impatiently.

"She says the children here in this room are all with various disabilities or infected with HIV/AIDS. Their parents had discarded them in garbage bins or by the side of roads as they are too ugly or sick to be raised up. They have become too numerous and the orphanage has run out of room, food and other essentials to take care of them. She says these are the excrement of society and they are no better than the rats which infect the institution. They are un-persons."

"But she is paid to take care of these children," I protested.

Strugurescu continued translating.

"She says that if you pay her American wages then she would take care of these children like in an American orphanage."

"Do you have medicine for these children?"

I had no sooner asked this question when I felt the utter foolishness of it.

"Medicine?" the nurse laughed. "Can't you see there are not even washing facilities here? The roof leaks and we have not been paid for the last six months. What do we feed our families at home, I would like to know! We used to think that these children were a source of income to us but not anymore. Don't talk to us about medicine for them. Let me take you upstairs and show you another thousand of these children. As you saw yourself, they are no better than food for rats."

Strugurescu and I looked at one another in consternation.

"Shall we continue?" the head nurse asked.

We were too dazed to reply and mechanically followed her starched skirt out. The door slammed shut behind us.

"I will now take you upstairs!" she said.

We nodded, our senses reeling from the shocking, benumbing sight behind us.

The head nurse took us to another room where the children were a little older. The room had more light, but heavy metal bars were everywhere. There were bars on the beds, the doors, and the windows.

"Look over there," I whispered to Strugurescu. "There are two kids tied to their beds! I can't make out whether it's bed sheets or rope! But their bones seemed deformed. It's like they grew up in the metal crib without ever leaving it."

In another part of the room, three children sat on a bench. I could tell that one of them had the palsy as he was shaking uncontrollably. Another was flapping his hands repetitively. The third twitched painfully as he dug his thumbs periodically into his eye sockets.

The head nurse saw me observing them.

"Those over there are alright. They are not going to hurt themselves. Others we have to tie down to prevent them from hurting themselves. If we don't, they bite themselves or hurl themselves at the concrete walls. If they are tied up, they do not get hurt."

"But if you tie them up, they will feel nothing either," I said.

She did not answer but walked off to view her charges. I noticed that she did not touch anyone.

"These are children not animals," I breathed to Strugurescu. "There must be something we can do to help them."

"If you have enough money, you can buy them," Strugurescu whispered back. "Maybe 10-20,000 dollars will buy one! I hear they are sold all the time. Shh! She's coming back."

"You have to go now," the head nurse said. "When these children see new people they tend to act out."

"But we have only seen two rooms," I said. "There must be more rooms."

"Yes, there are," the nurse replied. "But those rooms are for really sick children. You cannot enter those rooms."

I shuddered at the thought of what 'really sick' meant.

＠＜＠

27. A Discussion on Orphans

We took deep breaths as we emerged into the bright sunlight. The orphanage was a living nightmare. It was like nothing I had ever seen before.

"That was an experience!" I said. "I have never seen such total neglect in my entire life. I cannot believe that babies are wrapped and tied up like that to prevent them from moving or feeling!"

"You wanted to see an orphanage, remember?" Strugurescu replied. "There are many more orphanages exactly like this one all over Romania."

"I didn't know it was going to be that bad. By the way, why are there so many orphans here in this country?"

"They are actually not orphans. Most of them have parents. They are just left here because they are unwanted."

"But why would the parents leave their children in such wretched and squalid institutions?"

"It is not so easy for you to understand. You have to go back to Ceausescu's 1966-1967 social experiment to create a New Man."

"You mean, like the Nazi superman-Atlantis Aryan race?"

"No, not like that exactly. But Ceausescu wanted a new generation that would worship him and him alone."

"I see, a new generation that has no past memories, only the memory of him exclusively."

"Yes, you got it. So he decreed in 1966 that all women's uteruses belonged to the state. All women less than 40 years of age were encouraged and many times forced to have babies. Fetuses were the property of the entire society. Abortions and contraceptives were banned. In addition, a 10% celibacy tax on monthly wages was imposed on women who were not pregnant. As a result, in the next five years, more than two million children were born. These children were known as 'children of the decree'."

"As a Christian, I can understand about not wanting abortions but how can you control the uterus of a woman? I mean, it's not like you can make a woman have babies."

"Yes, you can. It is simple."

"I would like to see how you can do that to an American woman!"

"We are not talking about America. This is Romania. Ceausescu would reward mothers who were very productive with titles like 'Heroine Mother', 'Maternal Glory', and other maternity medals depending on the number of children the mother has."

"How many children does a mother need to have in order to earn 'Heroine Mother' status?" I asked curiously.

"More than ten! The family would also get more rations of food and other essentials."

"Sounds like a computer game. Only in this case, more babies get you to a higher level of food reward. So if you have a small family, you may starve?"

"That's it. But that's not all. Ceausescu would have medical doctors visit huge state run factories regularly. They were to check on the women workforce for pregnancies."

"That's not so bad. Free gynecological exams!"

"You misunderstand. These women were on a forced breeding program. You see, many of these pregnant women did not want to be pregnant in the first place. But with no contraceptives, they became pregnant and consequently, resort to back-alley or self abortions. They would stab their fetuses with knitting needles or inject their uterus with mustard and other juices to kill the baby. Back-alley abortions by unqualified doctors killed more than 10,000 women during this period. To prevent such practices, doctors were ordered to visit the factories, record the pregnancies, and then if any pregnant woman were to be caught later on trying to abort a fetus, they would be severely punished. Remember, Ceausescu wanted babies. Therefore, women would have babies whether they wanted to or not. After birth, many mothers would place their unwanted new born babies in state run orphanages for the state to take care of them. Sort of like 'since-you-wanted-it-so-you-take-care-of-it' attitude."

I was astonished. "That's the first Born-To-Order-Baby-Making-Machine story that I have ever heard."

"Exactly! But because of the numerous failed attempts at self or illegal abortions, many of these babies became severely disabled or handicapped when born. These unwanted and deformed babies were stigmatized and left to die in garbage heaps or thrown in the forests for the wolves to devour. After communism fell, one human rights organization, Terre des Hommes, led by Hans Hunick discovered a mass grave for children the size of four football fields! Nobody cared for the disabled babies as there were still thousands and thousands of healthy unwanted babies. Also, since communism was supposed to be the perfect system, handicapped children had to be hidden somewhere. This attitude of abandoning babies, handicapped or not, continues to this day. That is why there are so many 'orphans' here - children who are not wanted by their parents get dumped and institutionalized. Nowadays, it's mainly gypsies who abandon their babies."

"I did notice that their skins were darker in color. But then again, the head nurse told us that there were no washing facilities so it could just as well be layers of dirt on them."

"They are gypsies, believe me. I read somewhere that about 80% of abandoned babies are gypsies. Their culture allows and even encourages them to get married at twelve years of age or younger. Some become prostitutes at that early age. Then when they have babies, many of these child-mothers treat their babies like garbage. Not entirely their fault though as their unformed young breasts cannot even produce milk to nurture their babies. So the babies get dumped, just like the stray dogs, continuing the tradition when hundreds of thousands of mothers dumped their babies for the state to take care of them in Ceausescu's time. No wonder the nurses hit such children for pleasure."

"Isn't that illegal?"

"Probably, but who is going to know? Ever since the fall of Communism, I have heard that many young orphans have been physically and sexually abused by foreign pedophiles."

"Are you serious?"

"Yes, I'm serious. Foreigners from Western Europe, and even America, travel all the way here to have paid sex with little boys and girls. The nurses turn a blind eye as long as they are paid. I am sure that many of these children were also sold abroad as sex slaves. I told you – maybe ten, twenty thousand dollars and you can own your own child sex slave! Of course, many children do it voluntarily. That little girl you met yesterday and the hundreds, maybe thousands more little boys and girls living in the sewers, sell themselves to foreigners everyday. They have sex behind bushes in the parks, in seedy motel rooms, and even in specially arranged taxis which drive around in circles while the pedophile and the child have sex in the back seat."

"What you are telling me is incredible!"

"We, as a nation, did not even know that homosexuals and pedophiles existed until after 1989 when Romania's borders opened up. What you people take as natural has never been seen here before."

"Wait a second. I did not say it was natural."

"Yes, but you are different. You are a missionary."

"Is it only orphans that get such bad treatment?" I asked.

"No, of course not. Some parents, especially in the villages, sell their children like animals. A child, depending on sex and age, will fetch many times what a cow will fetch. Many times the child is forced into slavery or prostitution. The younger the child the higher the price!"

I grew sick. "Don't the authorities do anything about this?"

"Are you crazy? The authorities are powerless and corrupt. The gangs who ply this trade intimidate them or pay them off. I hear that child prostitution is extremely profitable."

"Isn't anybody honest here?" I asked.

"It's not about honesty, it's about unwanted children and also about fear and control," Strugurescu remarked. "Communism did this to us. It destroyed how we think and who we were."

28. Perescu's Picnic

After a few months in Romania, one of my neighbors on the tenth floor invited me out for a picnic. His name was Perescu.

Perescu was sixteen years old and must have had inherited genes from a pear as he was the exact shape of a pear. He was one of the friendliest guys I have ever met. Always with a positive outlook on life, he was in high school and eager to practice his English.

"My mum's invited you out for a picnic," he said cheerily.

"I accept," I said a little too quickly.

Now, a picnic may not sound like much but after many months of living in a strange land and always wondering where to find food, it meant a lot to me. My mouth watered envisioning barbecued ribs and sweet corn.

The day eventually came. Bright sunshine and a cool breeze made for a perfect day. I had inquired earlier whether I had to bring something. Perescu had informed me politely that all I had to bring was myself. I liked the sound of that very much for I had nothing to bring.

We met outside the block of flats.

"This is my mother and sister," Perescu said proudly.

The mother looked exactly like Perescu while his sister, about nine years of age, was as thin as a matchstick.

"Are you Jackie Chan?" she asked, wide eyed with curiosity.

"No, I'm not," I replied.

She sounded disappointed. "Then you must know Jackie Chan!"

"I do not know Jackie Chan," I said. "He's a famous movie star."

"Oh!" she said. And with that, lost all interest in me.

The mother chirped like a bird in a singing competition.

"I brought all the food," she sang cheerfully, showing two stuffed plastic bags. "I hope you are hungry."

I drooled. "Where are we going for the picnic? Do you need a lift there?"

"No car necessary," she sang. "It's right around the corner."

I thought that she meant the barbeque pits commonly seen around apartment blocks back in America. Strangely I had never seen a barbeque pit yet in Romania, less one around the corner! But I followed Perescu's mother - around the corner, then around another three corners, across a street, across a busy highway, finally to stop on the other side, at a railway-line embankment. The highway ran parallel to the train tracks with the small strip of grass in between.

"Here we are," Perescu said, throwing down the blankets.

"Are we staying here?" I asked. "We are sandwiched between trains and trucks. And there does not seem to be any pits here."

"We make one," Perescu replied.

I looked around. "How?"

"Just gather all the trash you can find. Then we'll light it and have a fire pit."

"Gather trash?"

"Yes, there's trash everywhere, especially along the tracks. Look for discarded oily things. Those burn the best."

I thought about the food and I thought about the fire. No fire, no food. Oh well, I thought, and started scrounging around the rail tracks for discarded pieces of paper, plastic, and wood.

When we got a nice fire going, Perescu's mother started preparing the food amid the honking of truck drivers and whistling of trains roaring by. First, she took out thick chunks of homemade bread and laid them beside the fire.

Then, as I waited eagerly for the ribs to appear, she popped out of her bags two glistening five-pound pieces of pure pork fat.

"Beautiful, no?" she asked.

I didn't know what to say.

She produced a knife from her skirt. I remembered Black Bear producing a nine-inch knife from his pants. I tried not to argue with people producing long knifes from their private parts.

She smiled and deftly cut the fat into slices which she skewered with a long, dead branch also procured from the rail tracks. Placing the fat on the roaring fire, she roasted the fat to a greasy, unctuous, dripping black mess. A hefty chunk of bread was then used to catch the dripping grease. When the bread became saturated, she gave it to Perescu.

Perescu, forever polite, turned around and offered me the lard sodden piece of bread.

"Here you go. Bon Appétit!"

I took the piece of bread, surprised by its weight. I figured that if I multiplied the mass of the lard the bread had absorbed by the gravitational pull of the earth, I will have enough oil to satisfy fifty years of The American Heart Association recommended daily intake of oils and fatty foods.

Perescu, his mother, and his sister all stopped and waited expectantly for me to pronounce judgment on this culinary delight. Their faces glowed from the bright flames.

Obligingly, I opened my mouth and bit into the bread.

Next moment, some of the oil either dripped or squirted out of my mouth and fell directly into the fire. The fire exploded with a powerful whoosh and the fresh bread laid out beside it began to burn brightly.

Perescu and his family rushed forward to rescue the bread as I retreated in the opposite direction - all the while thinking of ways to dispose of the piece of bread that was now attached to my hand like a limp wet appendage. I thought of throwing it like a Frisbee, but it would probably not fly.

The chunks of bread rescued, Perescu and his family got busy making and swallowing hot lard.

I nibbled on my slice slowly, choking on the fatty globs as it dribbled down my throat.

"We have to go collect more trash," Perescu said.

"Fine," I said quickly. "I'll guard the fire."

The moment Perescu and his family were out of sight, I chucked the piece of bread into the fire. There was a momentary burst of light, followed by dense black smoke.

The evidence was consumed.

I smiled innocently and politely declined more when the fire was stoked again with fresh trash. When the ten pounds of fat were devoured, Perescu's mother produced a small bottle.

"Would you like some?" she asked politely.

I was terribly hungry and I thought a little water would help calm my stomach.

"Sure! Give me a cup."

"You want a whole cup?"

"Yes, I want a full cup."

She stared at me strangely. "I'll give you a little first."

I didn't know why she was so stingy with the water. But I accepted it anyway.

"How is it?" she asked.

I tried to answer her, but found I was physically unable. What I just drank was no water at all, but some liquid powerful enough to take a rocket to the moon.

"This is not water!" I exclaimed.

"No, it's not," Perescu chipped in. "It's called Tuica. My family brews it in the village and they love it strong. We make it from prunes and other fruits. Sometimes we use it to degrease engines, too."

I figured that was how they degreased the lard in their bodies too.

"It is too strong for me. What's the percentage of alcohol in it? Thirty to forty percent like vodka?"

"Nobody drinks that weak Russian stuff," Perescu scoffed. "Our tuica is sixty percent alcohol. Only real men drink Tuica. Even my mother can drink a liter of it per day."

I looked down at the small cup in my hands and started wondering about my manliness.

29. Corrupt Doctors

A few weeks after the picnic, I was awakened by the telephone.

"I think my mother is dying," Perescu's voice came through on the line.

I rubbed the sleep from my eyes and replied stupidly. "What do you mean you think you're mother is dying? Don't you know for sure?"

"This is not a joke," Perescu said. "I would not call you at two in the morning for that. My mother has a terrible pain in her side and she was wondering if you could come up to our apartment and check on her. She is on the floor, bent in two."

I sat straight up, all sleep vanished in an instant. "I will drive your mother to the Emergency Room (ER) right now."

There was silence at the other end of the line.

"Hello!" I said. "Are you there?"

"Yes. My mother says that she does not want to go to the hospital. She says that hospitals in Romania are places where you go to die, not where you go to get healed."

"Are you going to listen to me or to her? That type of pain could mean a ruptured appendix or gall bladder. She could die if not treated immediately."

There was silence for a long time. "My mother says that she feels better now and that there is no need for you to even come."

"Tell your mother that unless she goes to the ER, I will call the ambulance to get her."

I could hear spirited arguments in the background.

The Perescu's voice came back. "She still does not agree. Give me a few minutes to talk to her. In the meantime, why don't you call the ambulance?"

I dialed Emergency immediately. It rung forever before a voice came on.

"Do you speak English?" I shouted.

A smattering of words sounded from the other side which I took to mean a 'possible yes'.

"Can you send an ambulance to this address?" I read the address over the phone.

More chatter emanated from the other end. After another eternity of waiting, a sad voice came back.

"No ambulance."

"No ambulance?" I asked in amazement. "But this is an EMERGENCY! You must have an ambulance."

"No petrol for ambulance," the voice said sorrowfully. "We cannot drive with no petrol."

"You-have-no-petrol-for-your-ambulance," I said slowly. "And this is the Emergency Ward?"

"Yes," the voice replied mournfully. "No petrol for ambulance until next month. No petrol, no ambulance."

I could not argue with such profound logic. I rang Perescu back.

"How's your mother?"

"I talked some sense into her. She's willing to go in the ambulance."

"Change of plans. I will drive you there. Meet me in the parking lot in five minutes."

Five minutes later we were speeding towards the ER. Perescu's mother was bundled up in a cocoon of blankets. She was lying prone in the back seat, her face whiter than a dead albino seal. It was not a good sign. Thankfully, Perescu's sister was with some relatives and not present to witness her mother's stint with death.

"Maybe it's just heartburn," I suggested to Perescu. "All the pure fat that she eats! Or maybe her overworked gall bladder, bile ducts, or liver gave up and burst."

That brought a burst of worried screams from the back.

"She did not eat any lard today," Perescu translated. "Shhh! She understands the word 'bile'."

I bit down on my tongue and focused on my driving. In my mind, I envisioned lard and moonshine Tuica duking it out in her body. The roads were empty and we reached the ER in record time. I drove up to the entrance and helped Perescu roll his mother out and into the waiting room.

I parked the car and rushed back to the waiting room.

The room was about twenty-seven by nine feet. My first thought when I walked in was that unbeknownst to me, Romania had been invaded by Russia and the wounded had been brought to the hospital. The room was packed with patients. A few were sitting, some were standing listlessly, while others were lying on the floor.

"Get a nurse," I yelled at Perescu.

"There are no nurses here!" Perescu said.

"That's impossible. There must be a nurse here."

"There are nurses here," Perescu said.

"You just told me that there were no nurses here! You're making no sense!"

"You don't understand. What I meant was that there are nurses here in the ER but they are not going to help us until we pay them."

"Pay them?" I said incredulously. "Why do we have to pay them?"

"So that they will take you in to see the doctor. If we do not pay, we can wait here until we die."

"How much should we pay them?" Suddenly I understood why there were so many unattended patients in the waiting room.

"A few dollars should suffice."

"Why don't you pay them then?"

Perescu fidgeted.

"What's wrong now?" I asked impatiently.

"The nurse will only take you in to see the doctor," Perescu said.

"Isn't that what we want?"

"Yes, but then we have to pay the doctor too. Otherwise he will not look at my mother."

"Doesn't your mother have state insurance care?"

"Yes, she has, but you have to pay the doctor extra."

"What happens if we pay the doctor, but not the nurse?"

"The nurses will drop her on the floor."

"We don't want that."

"Anyway, we cannot get in to pay the doctor without going through the nurses."

"So you have to pay the state, pay the nurses, and then pay the doctor before somebody will see your mother?'

"Basically, yes. That is how it works here. If there is a receptionist, then we have to pay her too. And the orderlies as well…and when they see you, as a foreigner, we may have to pay triple!"

"Have you tried prayer?" I asked.

The comment was lost on Perescu and his mother.

At that time, a nurse walked out into the waiting room. A sea of faces, some deformed with pain, turned to plead with her.

"The doctor has gone out," she informed all of us. "He will be back but we do not know when."

"Probably gone home," Perescu murmured to me. "He will not return tonight."

"Please can we go back home," Perescu's mother pleaded softly. She was crying more from shame than from pain. "We don't have enough money to pay all the nurses, and the doctor as well. And if we need an X-ray, the technician will also ask for money. I told you we shouldn't have come in the first place. If I die, at least let me die at home."

We left with some of the other patients. Others hung on to the hope that the doctor would return as they had no other place to go to. Upon reaching home, I gave Perescu's mother some pain relieving tablets in the hope that it would reduce her pain. Thankfully, Perescu's mother recovered fully from that crisis and continues to eat enormous quantities of lard and drink enormous quantities of moonshine to this day.

The sad state of corruption in public hospitals in Romania continues to hound patients without money. In 2009, an elderly woman from Satu Mare, a city in the northwestern part of Romania, died shortly after being sent from door to door, hospital to hospital as she could not afford to pay the bribes required to receive treatment. There exists an unwritten list of bribes. A simple appendix removal requires a bribe of US$130 while complicated surgeries require bribes of many thousands of dollars. This is tacitly agreed upon by the doctors. Also in 2009, a whole hospital in the northeastern part of Romania was put under investigation after rampant reports of coerced payments by doctors and staff. A patient who is unable to come up with the required bribe, is doomed from the start.

Perescu's mother was right, hospitals are places where you go to die, or go broke, whichever comes first.

æ∞⊄

30. The Gentle Art of Lying

A week later, the phone woke me up again. Only this time it was not Perescu but a hollow voice.

"Your friend came and removed the equipment. I hope that was OK."

It took me awhile to recognize that the hollow voice belonged to the guard at the discotheque.

"What are you trying to say?" I asked in surprise.

"Your friend dropped by this morning and picked up all the equipment. He said you were rehearsing again and that you needed the instruments."

I sat bolt upright in my bed.

"I didn't instruct any such thing! Who was it that took the instruments?"

"The boy who was with you before - the one with the round moon face!"

"You mean Telemescu, the music student?"

"I think that was his name. He was with you when you rented this place. And he was with you all the time when you practiced here. I know his face very well. He said you asked him to take the instruments. So I opened the room for him."

I was breathing hard. "Is he still there? If he is stop him immediately!"

"He left sometime ago."

"Why didn't you call me earlier to check to see whether it was OK or not? I thought I told you not to open the room for anyone but me."

"He was with you before! He was always with you when you came here. So I thought it must be alright to release the equipment."

I didn't know what to think. I thought I had been explicit in my instructions. I quickly called Telemescu.

He answered after the first two rings. I breathed a sigh of relief.

"Thank God you are there!" I exhaled. "Why did you take all the equipment? Are you rehearsing something?"

There was silence on the other end. Then Telemescu spoke quietly.

"What equipment?"

"The one that you took from the locked room at the discotheque!"

"I didn't take anything from there," Telemescu said.

"Are you telling me that you did not go to the discotheque and take out all the equipment early this morning?"

"I was at the Conservatory all morning. I am still at the Conservatory."

"The guard told me that you had been there and had removed all the instruments!"

"I wasn't there. The guard is lying. Why don't we go over there and see the guard?"

"OK, I can meet you at the discotheque in an hour."

I dressed, rushed out, and promptly collided with Mrs. Urdescu on the landing outside.

"Excuse me!" I said. "I didn't see you."

"You cannot park your car here," Mrs. Urdescu began.

I didn't quite understand what she meant. "What do you mean I cannot park my car here? I parked in the common parking lot. I always park it there - in any available spot. I live here so I park here!"

"A free parking spot does not mean that it is available for you to park there."

"There were many free parking spots. I just parked in one. Does it matter?"

"People are angry with you for parking here!" Mrs. Urdescu bellowed. "You and your car do not belong here."

I didn't know what to say. I gritted my teeth.

"I have some very important things to do right now. Maybe we can continue this talk later."

I dashed down the stairs before Mrs. Urdescu had a chance to open her mouth to retaliate. I ran to my car and...stopped in horror at the sight of my little Aro.

Somebody had thrown a large can of brown paint all over the car in the night. Its bright gold color was now spotted with a multitude of dark brown spots. I had been 'dalmationized'!

I was reeling from this sight when Perescu, my friendly neighbor from the picnic, walked by.

"What happened to your car?" Perescu asked, his eyes popping at the sight of the brown mess.

"I don't know what happened," I replied in anguish. "I just came out and found it this way!"

"I think I know what happened," Perescu said.

"What happened?" I asked in astonishment. "Did you see who did this?"

"No, I did not."

"Then how do you know what happened?"

"This happens quite frequently. If you park in somebody's place they will throw a can of paint over your car! It serves as a warning sign."

"But all these places are free!"

Perescu's face took on a wiser-than-thou look.

"Yes, they are free but they are not."

This was the second time I have heard this mysterious phrase.

"What do you mean?"

"People who have been living here for forty-fifty years reserve parking places for themselves."

"But they have no cars!" I nearly screamed.

"It does not matter. They have been here longer so they consider the place to be theirs and you have no right to park in their places."

"They could have just told me and I would have moved my car willingly."

"They don't talk to foreigners here," Perescu said. "They don't trust them."

"How do I find out who did this?" I asked.

"You can't. The person who reserved this spot will never admit to it!"

"Thanks for the information," I said. "I'll have to solve this later as I really have to go meet someone now."

"Are you going to drive your car with all that paint on it?" Perescu sounded shocked.

"I have no choice!"

Perescu must have found this extremely funny for he proceeded to laugh himself silly as I drove off in my spotted car.

....

I drove straight to the discotheque amid curious stares from passers-by. Telemescu, his face blank, was waiting for me. We quickly found the incensed guard.

"What happened this morning?" I asked the guard.

"That's the boy who came this morning and took all the equipment!" the guard shouted, pointing at Telemescu.

"What do you mean?" Telemescu shouted back. "I told you I wasn't here this morning. I was in school."

"He took all your things!" the guard said. "He's a thief!"

"Shut up, you drunk! You are the thief. Look at your drunken red face and bloodshot eyes! Anybody can tell that you took all the equipment yourself and am trying to blame it on me. Did you sell it all for more alcohol?"

"You liar!" the guard screamed.

"You no-good drunk!" Telemescu screamed back.

"Can we see the room?" I asked quietly.

"What's the use of seeing the room?" the guard bawled. "Your thieving friend here removed everything already. Students are poor so they steal all the time."

"You stole it to buy more alcohol!" Telemescu bawled back. "You stink of liquor!"

"I'll show you the empty room," the guard roared. "After that I will call the police on him. He has an angelic face but the heart of the devil!"

"Call the police," Telemescu roared back. "Let them take you to the station. They will see that the veins on your face and eyes are leaking alcohol! Let's see whom they will believe."

They continued hurling insults at each other as the guard shuffled over and opened the door of the room. I stepped in.

I had prayed for some miracle but there was none. The room was cleaned out. All my musical instruments and equipment worth US$6,000 had disappeared!

"I would never steal your equipment," Telemescu whispered to me. "I want to help you."

"He stole all of your equipment," the guard stated matter-of-factly. "I have no reason to lie to you. Let us call the police."

"Yes, let us call the police," Telemescu reaffirmed.

I didn't know who to believe as we waited for the police. When they finally arrived, the guard and Telemescu each gave their side of the story. The police wanted to find out who owned the equipment.

"Are you the owner?" they asked me.

"Yes, I am."

"Seeing that you are a foreigner, we cannot help you further!"

"Why? Aren't you supposed to help?"

"You can seek help from your embassy. We are the local police and we do not interfere when foreigners are robbed or swindled. Anyway, foreigners can afford losses since they all have money!"

"The embassy is not going to help me on this matter," I protested. "They have other state matters to deal with. And not all foreigners are rich!"

"That is all we can do. We do not have the resources to help foreigners. We have not been paid for three months. Our colleagues are on strike. We have taken statements from everybody concerned. If your equipment shows up, we will inform you."

They turned around and left. I stared at their departing backs.

"Your round face friend stole it," the guard huffed as he walked away. "He's a thief and a liar! What's the point in going to school? You don't need to go to school to become a thief!"

"You don't know what you are saying, you drunk!" Telemescu shouted back and walked out.

I was in a real quandary. Either of them could be lying. There was no way to find out. Or worse, they could both be acting but actually, in cahoots to swindle me. It was impossible to tell. There was nothing else for me to do but drive back home in my spotted car.

31. Enter Christ

I spent the next few days cleaning the Aro of its spots and wondering where I was going to find the money to replace all the musical instruments which had been stolen. About that same time, Strugurescu who was now back in the army, called.

"Do you know anybody who would be interested in buying the Aro?" I asked, after a few minutes of idle chatter.

"Well, I would like to buy it, but I just don't have the money," Strugurescu said. "However, I have a brother who might be interested. I heard him telling my mother, before I went back to the army that he wanted to buy a car. He has enough money to buy your car easily."

I could have kissed him.

"Give me his name and telephone number and I will call him."

"He works in a bar so I will give you the number for the bar. He has been with them for the last five years. He sort of runs the place for his boss."

He gave me his brother's name and number.

I called Strugurescu's brother the moment I got off the line. His name was Christnescu. I informed him that I was a friend of his brother and asked for an appointment. He was cordial

and more importantly, interested in the Aro. We set up a
meeting at five at his work place.

....

The air was difficult to breathe because the cigarette smoke
was so thick. Communist brands filled the air intermingled
with the recognizable smell of Marlboros. A dingy red light
hung behind even more dingy curtains that half hid the
American cowboy icon. The bar itself was camouflaged with
smoke. Even the tables and chairs had taken on a pale grey-
ash texture. Some shadowy figures were shooting pool at a
shadowy table in the background. There were a few drunks at
the bar.

Christnescu came out from behind the bar the moment he
saw me. He was short, plump, well dressed, and wore a
permanent tiny smile on his face. We shook hands and sat
down on the ethereal grey chairs.

"So you know my brother Strugurescu?"

"Yes! I know him quiet well."

"Do you want a drink?"

"No, I don't drink."

"What is he up to these days?"

"Don't you know? He's back in the army."

"We are not so close," Christnescu replied. "By the way,
call me Christ!"

"It was your brother who mentioned that you might be
interested in my Aro."

"He's right, I do want to buy one. I love to travel and that small SUV is just what I need. It is also good in the city as the holes in the streets here are sometimes worse than the bed streams in the villages."

We laughed at that.

"When it rains here in the city, the gargantuan holes get filled with water and become invisible," I added. "You only know it's there when your car disappears into the hole."

"That's why I want to buy an SUV," Christ said. "By the way, why do you want to sell it?"

"Somebody stole all my equipment and music instruments I had for starting a ministry. I am selling the car to replace the stolen stuff. It's a new car and I just had it for a short while. It runs well. With this sale, I will be able to replace the stolen equipment."

Christ's eyes popped out of his head. He sat up straight.

"This city is filled with crooks! I will help you! I come from a large denominational church myself. I will buy your car. Don't worry; you will replace all you have lost."

I was overwhelmed with gratitude.

"Don't you want to know how much the car is?"

"How much is it?"

I told him the price.

"I can afford that," Christ said confidently. "I have saved up over the years."

"If you want to see the car, it is right outside the bar."

We went out to inspect the car. It took him only a few seconds to eyeball the car and express his approval.

"What do you think?" I asked.

"I'll take it," Christ replied. He reached into his pocket and fished out US$500. "That will be my down payment on the car. Since you know my brother, I will trust you. Also, since you are a Christian, I will help you. When you have finished with the transfer papers, I will give you the rest of the money. That way, you can replace all of your equipment. Here is my personal mobile number. Call me when you are done with the papers."

"I will."

We shook hands and I walked out of the bar $500 richer than when I walked in.

"Praise you Jesus!" I said. "And thank-you Christ!"

I completed the transfer papers in the next few days.

32. Exit Christ

Christ lived with his mother, in a small house with high fences, on the outskirts of the city. It had taken me more than an hour, navigating through narrow streets, to get there.

A squat woman with her hair tightly bundled up in a shawl, Christ's mother ushered me into her tiny living room and promptly served me cakes and tea. I demurred but was forcefully overruled. After she was sure that I had tasted all her delicacies, she left to care for her squealing pigs in the courtyard.

I looked around the room. It was cluttered but tidy at the same time. Three Bibles stood on the window sill and one more delicately balanced the television so that it stayed level. The sun shone brightly through the gaily patterned curtains and made a clean swath of the room. There was no dust.

I looked impatiently at the clock on the wall. It read 5:00 pm. Christ had told me to meet him at his home to seal the deal for the car. He should have been home by now.

The minutes slowly ticked by.

At 6:00 pm, Christ's mother dropped by to check on my condition. She could not understand why I was still waiting for her son. She forced some more of her delicious cakes on me and grumbled about the tardiness of her son. Then her chickens clucked and she had to rush out to check on them.

By 7:00 pm, Christ's mother was crying and apologizing for her son's behavior. She tried to tell me that her son worked very late sometimes and would not be home before two or three in the morning. She blamed the owner of the bar for keeping her son working so late. She confided to me that she was very worried about the bad influence the bar could have on her son. To entertain me, she sang some hymns from a hymnal. Then it was time to bring the cows home and she disappeared again.

It was completely dark by 8:00 pm. Christ's mother was all dithery and flustered that her son was still not home. I got worried too. I had driven over when it was still light. I was sure that I would get lost trying to navigate the back streets to the city.

At that precise moment, Christ called. Her mother handed me the phone.

"When are you getting here?" I asked. "I have been here since five and your mother is worried sick about you."

"I'm sorry that I cannot come right now," Christ replied. "The boss has me running around re-supplying and re-stocking the whole place. I do not know when I can get out. Please leave the car with my mother and I will test it tonight when I get back home. Then you can come back early next morning for the money."

I turned around and explained all this to his mother.

"I'm going to leave the Aro here tonight in the yard. Here are the keys. I cannot wait anymore. Christ can test it when he comes back home. I'm calling a taxi to take me back home but I'll be back tomorrow at six or seven in the morning to meet Christ before he goes to work."

The mother promised to tell her son everything I had said. She begged my forgiveness for her son's tardiness as the taxi pulled away.

....

Bright and early the next day, I took a taxi back to Christ's house. I knocked on the high gates and waited. Nobody answered. I looked at my watch. It showed 6 am. Christ and his mother should be home. Of course, they could still be asleep. I knocked louder and succeeded in rousing a neighbor living across the street.

"Who are you looking for?" he shouted across the gate.

"I'm looking for Christ," I said. "Do you know whether he's home?"

The neighbor walked over.

"Christ doesn't live here! Only his mother lives here."

"I met his mother yesterday. Christ told me that he would be home by 5:00 pm but he got delayed. Are you sure he does not live here?"

"Of course I am sure! I have been here fifty years."

"If he doesn't live here, I will just take my car and leave. I can meet him somewhere else later."

"What car?" the neighbor asked. "They do not have a car."

"I left a car here last night. It was for Christ to test before he bought it."

The neighbor pointed to a slit in the high fence. "There's no car there! Look for yourself."

I peered through the crack. Sure enough, the yard was empty.

"Maybe Christ is testing the car right now," I prayed. That would account for the car's absence.

The neighbor stared at me, turned around without a single word, and walked back into his house. His gate clicked shut purposefully behind him.

It was the longest wait of my life. My heart hammered in my chest. I gulped in air and prayed scripture. That helped calmed me down. Then a fresh streak of doubt swept through my mind and my heart started pounding painfully again. Where was the car? Why was there no one home? Did something happen? After five hours I gave up waiting. All the knocking had produced no results. Nobody answered. Even the pigs and chickens remained quiet. I walked back to the main road, caught a taxi, and arrived back home.

The first thing I did was to call Christ's mobile phone number but there was no answer. I must have tried a hundred times before I dialed the number for the bar. Somebody answered and informed me that Christ was unavailable. But I wanted to be sure, so I took a taxi down to the bar. The place looked just as decrepit as when I first saw it. I walked in and immediately spied Christ at the back of the bar.

"Christ!" I shouted.

Christ looked up, saw who it was and bolted for the back door. He shot out so fast that I began to doubt whether it was really him. I walked up to the smoky pool table where two men were lounging.

"Was that Christ?" I asked. "I have to talk to him."

"Why do you want to talk to him?" the first man asked.

"He stole my car."

"Your car?" the second man interjected. "He told me it was his new car!"

"Shut up!" the first man snarled. He slid a cigarette out, a Marlboro, tapped it, and put it between his lips.

"We don't know about any car but you should know that Christ works for the Russian mafia. You should be very careful about who you are accusing."

I didn't know whether he was threatening or warning me.

"Does Christ live around here?" I asked. "I have to talk to him."

"If he wants to talk to you, he will call you."

I swallowed painfully. "Tell him that I am looking for him."

I could feel their eyes boring into my back as I walked out of the bar.

33. Wild, Wild, West Lawyers

The waiting room was aesthetically decorated befitting the seriousness of his profession. Black leather couches tastefully blended with the dark mahogany wood on the walls and furniture. An aura of respectability and righteousness surrounded the pleasant secretary who had politely informed me that the lawyer would be with me shortly. Coffee and tea were offered, for which I was very thankful. The decorum would have passed muster in the most venerated law offices in America.

I leaned back comfortably in the plush leather seat and thought about the events that had led me here. A pleasant voice soon jerked me out of my reverie.

"The lawyer will see you now," the secretary purred.

I was led into an inner office which was even more expensively furnished. Palatial old Italian desks mixed with colonial British period couches were the theme of the inner sanctum. But what struck me most was the lawyer himself. He stood over six-foot tall and weighed correspondingly. To say he was imposing would be an understatement. He was a monument!

"How can I help you?" he said in a baritone voice.

"I need your help in recuperating some stolen property of mine," I replied.

"Have you been to the police?"

"The police have not been very helpful."

"I understand. Please tell me what happened and what you want recovered."

I launched into my stories of what happened to my car and the musical equipment.

"I have all the receipts for the equipment and the title of the car with me." I pushed a file containing the papers over.

He perused the papers carefully, leaned back in his chair, and lit up a cigarette.

"You are not the first foreigner to be tricked. This has happened many, many times before. There are many tricksters in this country. The police can't be bothered with such crimes as it involves foreigners. I believe your story not only because you have all the relevant documents but I happen to know my countrymen very well."

"What I want to know is whether you can help me or not," I said in earnest.

"We *can* get your equipment, instruments and car back," the lawyer said, without a trace of hesitation.

I smiled for the first time in a very long time. The smile must have touched both my ears. It was going to be easy after all. Thank God for lawyers.

The lawyer pressed his hands together in a paternalistic, Godfather-like manner.

"Like I said we can get all your stuff back. This is what you have to do."

I leaned in closer forgetting to breathe.

"You have to hire three guys to beat up Christ, Telemescu, and the guard. After they are beaten up half to death, they will give you back your car and your music equipment. I guarantee that. That is how we solve problems like this here in this country."

I stared at the lawyer dumfounded.

But he was not finished yet. In the absolute silence of the venerated office, he breathed stealthily and held up three fat fingers.

"I have three guys who would be willing to do the job for you. They have done this many times before. Shall I call them for you?"

"I hear Christ may be with the Russian mafia," I stammered.

"My boys have guns. We are not afraid of the Russians."

I breathed deeply. It was so tempting. Revenge would be so sweet. I wanted to shout 'Yes, oh please, YES!' so badly. But in my spirit, I could not see Jesus hiring three thugs to beat up and half-kill Christ, Telemescu, and the old guard.

I fidgeted uncomfortably. "I'm a missionary here and I'm afraid I cannot hire people to beat up other people."

"Then you will never see your car or equipment ever again."

"I choose to forgive them instead."

He shook his head. "You should teach them a lesson so that they will not cheat other people. If they begin to believe that they can do this 'tricks' without any consequence, they will just get bolder. But if that is your choice, then I'm afraid I cannot help you anymore."

He rose up from his leather seat, shook my hand, and ushered me out of his office. That was my last contact with the lawyer, Christ, Telemescu, the guard at the discotheque, all my musical equipment, and my little SUV.

34. Conversations with God II

I desperately needed my Father after these episodes.

"Everything seems to be going wrong," I complained. "I don't seem to be protected, doors are not opening, and resources are being stolen. I feel that I am in the wrong place. I feel so defeated."

"Are you interested in doing ministry or are you committed to doing ministry?"

"What's the difference?" I asked.

"There are many who are 'interested' in serving Me. They say 'Here am I, Lord! Send me!' They take the plunge into the unknown, travel on short term mission trips, serve in soup kitchens and on the streets. They volunteer at the local church. But after a period of serving, they discover that it is not always convenient or easy. Circumstances seem to be worse off. Their spirit gets tired and weary, even turning bitter and sour. They find themselves saying, "Where was God when we needed Him?" or "We gave so much and we got back nothing!" or "How could a loving God allow such a thing to happen?" They finally get disinterested in serving and give up. The flame which once burnt so brightly in them is now barely a flicker. Those are the 'interested' in ministry. They are only interested insofar as circumstances are ideal and problems are non-existent."

I felt a deep conviction in my heart. He had described me so well.

But He was not finished yet. "Yet there are others who seem to move beyond interested. They go through the same problems and challenges yet they maintain the initial passion and energy. Their flame continues to burn brightly. These are the 'committed'. They take the punches, roll through them, and continue forward. Year after year, they plod on. These are the people who fall but get up, the knocked down but not knocked out, the ones who drive through six feet of snow to get to church because they want to support their pastor. They help build and support the church through sacrificial giving. They have made a decision and are not allowing their emotions or adverse circumstances to stand in their way. They are invaluable to Me. So, are you committed to ministry or are you just interested in ministry?"

"Father, help me be committed," I cried.

"Also, develop your wisdom."

"What do you mean?" I asked.

"Your mistake was to trust people blindly, forgetting that trust has to be earned. Paul commanded Timothy, his student, to set an example for the believers. It was not just his talk but his walk that was important. In fact, it was far more important as many people will look at his walk and not at his talk. A person can tell you how good he is but until he proves it, it remains just words. You have been fooled because you have not tested the words spoken to you. You tend to trust too quickly. Integrity comes with time and is earned slowly. The life a person lives is more important than the words he speaks."

I realized I had a lot more to learn. I decided to change the topic.

"Father, what about the things that were stolen? Will you repay them seven times over? I am making nothing yet losing everything. What about the principle of sowing and reaping? I understand about the crowns in heaven but what about my rewards now? Isn't the laborer worthy of his wages?"

"There is a story from the book of Judges about a young Levite who has been well trained in priestly duties. He has worked hard and now expects to be compensated for his years of hard work. Finding nothing suitable in Bethlehem, he decided it was time to move out. He interviewed at many places but found none to his liking. The wages and the perks were just not good enough.

Then he heard of an opening at a questionable character's house - a man who was called Micah who wanted a priest and was willing and able to give a good salary plus benefits. The interview went very well. Both parties agreed on a win-win solution. In the end, Micah got a priest and the Levite ended up with a good financial package.

Many people in ministry are exactly like the young Levite in this story. They serve Me but only for 'money, clothes, and food'. If there is no money they will not serve. They take to the airwaves, they plead for more money, and they abandon congregations that do not pay them enough. They move to another place which offers them 'more money, more clothes, and more food'. And when another opportunity arises which gives them 'even more money, even more clothes, and even more food' they move to that new place. They envy other ministers with bigger ministries and talk bad about them.

They want the nicest buildings, the biggest ministries, and they talk about success incessantly.

Their congregation sees this and learns it. If they, in turn, are not blessed financially then they will leave the church. They will seek a more financially anointed church and pastor - somebody whom they think can call down My blessings upon them quicker. They envy their neighbors and friends who have more. When they pray, they ask that I bless their carefully laid down plans to make more money.

You cannot allow My call to be replaced by The job. The job is all about money. My call is not. Do you desire to only have a successful life or do you want a significant life? My Word has to be preached and shared whether you are compensated abundantly, adequately, not adequately, or not at all. My good news has to be preached in the loftiest castle as well as the humblest hut. For in doing a job, you are to be compensated monetarily. You will become successful. But for answering My call, and to become significant, I am your sufficient reward."

35. Credinescu, the Faithful

A few weeks after my encounter with the wild, wild, west lawyer, I made friends with Credinescu. He was from a nearby village and was blessed and cursed with good looks - blessed because his looks got him many female friends but cursed because having that many female friends caused him multiple headaches.

"I am going to start a non-denominational church," I informed Credinescu. "Would you like to help?"

His Hollywood good looks remained unfazed. "I have heard about non-denominational churches but do not know too much about them."

"Not any church, but a church that worships God freely and actively. We are going to stand up and worship God for an hour or so! I know it has never been done before in Romania."

"It has never been done before because nobody can or wants to stand up that long to worship God! People here are used to sitting down or if they stand it is not for worship."

"I am sure it can be done."

"It cannot be done! It goes against the culture and tradition of our country."

"I am not trying to go against the culture and tradition of your country. I am just trying to start a church that will worship and praise God freely in the Spirit. I am surprised that no other church has even considered that before."

"Oh! But the other churches are already aware of you and your intentions. The crusades you did before attracted some attention."

"Really? What do they say about me?"

"They are actively praying against you!" Credinescu blurted out.

I raised my eyebrows. "What do you mean they are actively praying against me?"

"Well, I have friends in other churches and they told me that their pastors are praying for your failure. Actually, their pastors are starting a campaign to pray against you. My friends told me they specifically prayed that your church, if it's started, will not last three months!"

"Well, that's something isn't it? At least they gave me three months!"

Credinescu warmed up. "Actually they only gave you a month. I told you three to make you feel better. My friends told me too that you will be rejected by the Romanians because you look different. No non-Romanian will ever be accepted as a pastor here!"

"You are such a good friend! By the way, what do you mean I look different?"

"Look around you. Do you see any other person who looks like you living here in this city? You are the only one! There are no other foreigners in this whole city!"

"So what?"

"So what?" Credinescu echoed. He stood up and proceeded to demonstrate 'so what' for me. "Imagine a person walking down the street."

"Okay..."

"He suddenly sees an insect in his way. The insect is new, unknown, and foreign. It is a type never seen before."

I imagined myself as the exotic never-before-seen insect.

"Well, that person is not going to approach the insect. He will give it a wide berth. Avoid it, inspect it from a distance, wait to see what harm that insect can do. Maybe kill the insect!"

I wondered how long I was going to last before somebody squashed me under their heel with relish.

"Now do you know what I am talking about when I say you look different?" Credinescu said, calming down and coming to sit by the insect, I mean, by my side, again.

"I see it very well," I mumbled, rubbing my antenna with concern. "You seem to know a lot about other churches and what they think. Can you tell me more?"

"Let me give you an analogy. Imagine a mighty tree. The trunk of that mighty tree is the Orthodox church. A very long time ago, a branch from that mighty tree grew bad, putrefied and fell off the tree. It fell some distance away from the tree. A rotten branch that split from its source! Well, that rotting branch is the Catholic church – as it split away from the Orthodox. On that decaying branch are some twigs. Those twigs are the Baptists, the Pentecostals, and all other evangelicals. And if you look very closely, you will discover that there is a very small thorn on one of the twigs. That thorn is you - the new non-denominational free-worship church!"

Well, I have been called many things in my life but this was new to me. A small irritating thorn on a dead twig on a rotten branch that lies some distance away from the living tree! Maybe I was the insect crawling on the thorn.

"I do not know very much about the Orthodox religion," I confessed. "Is it similar to the rotten branch, I mean, the Catholic faith?"

"Well, I am not too familiar with the Catholics but I can give you a brief summary of Orthodoxy as practiced here in Romania. By the way, I am not Orthodox but I have many Orthodox friends."

"Please tell me."

"The first thing you need to learn is that you are illegitimate."

"Me? Illegitimate?" I sputtered.

"Yes! No Christian outside the Orthodox faith is considered legitimate. The Orthodox consider themselves as the one and only true Christian church and faith. Also the Orthodox liturgy is considered to be the only right form of worship. That is why your style of worship is unacceptable. Chanting, the burning of incense and the singing of public prayers of the liturgy as opposed to private prayers are considered correct and the only acceptable way to worship God. Emulating heavenly beauty on earth is very important. If you enter an Orthodox church, you will find many beautiful gold icons. Also, the priests, deacons, sub-deacons, readers, cantors, and even doorkeepers are beautifully, and expensively, dressed."

This was all new to me. I remembered pastors in California who preach in loud Hawaiian casual shirts and polyester shorts. It was not the time to bring that up.

"Tell me more about the icons," I asked instead. "Doesn't the Bible forbid the worship of idols?"

"Well, there is the official teaching and then there is the actual practice," Credinescu pontificated wisely. "The holy icons in the Orthodox church are two dimensional, not 3D statues. So it can be claimed that they are not idols per se. Of course, anything can be an idol, not necessary statues. So the official position of the church is that they venerate the icons, but they do not worship them. But the practice of worshipping, prostrating, and kissing the icons is the norm. For all icons, saints, and relics are worshipped in practice because the belief is that God dwells in them and hence, they are worthy to be worshipped."

"Saints and relics?" I inquired.

"The Orthodox believe that God became man so that man might become God. Hence the worship of saints. And the relics are pieces of saint bones or a piece of their clothing. Those are highly coveted for worship purposes."

"I see."

"A few other beliefs, you might want to know is that baptism in sanctified water cleanses sin and that the Eucharist, which is performed a few times per year, is the real body and blood of Christ."

"That is the same as the Catholic belief," I pointed out. "But what about the worship of Mary?"

"The official teaching is that Mary is not worshipped, but venerated. She intercedes for those of the Orthodox faith. She is not a mediator between God and humanity but an advocate between humanity and her Son, Jesus Christ. Mary weeps for the sins of the world and on judgment day, she will ask her Son to pardon the world."

"What percentage of the population is Orthodox?" I asked, with interest.

"Probably ninety percent," Credinescu answered, without hesitation. "Maybe higher in other parts of the country."

"How about non-denominational, charismatic, free-worship churches?"

"None here in this city but you can be the first."

"In America, the largest churches are non-denominational," I insisted. "It is nothing new."

"This is Romania, not America. Here, if you do not belong to a denomination, you will be run out of town."

"I know all about running," I said enigmatically. "Maybe you would like to help me out? We could begin scouting for a place for church. It does not have to be a big place as I am not planning any more crusades."

Credinescu smiled. "You are insistent! I will be happy to help you start your church but you must realize that you will probably fail."

"Why would you want to help me considering that my failure is imminent?"

"Because I am willing to try something different."

"If you join me, then by association, you become the insect everybody wants to trample on."

Credinescu laughed heartily at that comment.

36. The Search Begins

Credinescu met me at 8:00 the next morning. He still wore a huge smile, a leftover from all that laughing he did yesterday.

"Are you ready?" I asked. "Today's the day!"

"Sure, I'm ready!" Credinescu said. "Let's go!"

Our first stop was a local high school with a big gymnasium. We went there by foot. As we approached the gym, we noted with consternation the weather-beaten coat of light green paint on the building. But we could see that it had bright lights and the windows appeared clean

"This place looks real ugly," Credinescu said. "The paint is peeling but it has lights and could serve us well."

"You're right," I agreed. "We could start out here and then move after a few months, to a better place."

Credinescu waved his hands emphatically. "This is a great, central location. People can walk here easily just like we did."

I nodded. "That is good since many people do not own a car. We would be right in the midst of the community."

"Let's go in, meet the school director, and sign the contract."

"Good idea. We could be home within the hour. After that, maybe we can go out and have some breakfast."

We walked confidently into the school. The hallways were empty except for a cleaning lady. After a short inquiry, she ushered us into the director's office.

The director was a man in his mid-forties. He smiled, got up, shook our hands, and even pulled chairs out for us. We thanked God in our hearts that the director was friendly.

"What can I do for you?" the director asked.

"We would like to rent your gym," Credinescu began.

"That is possible," the director said. "We rent out our gym to the community all the time. That way, we derive some income to help us maintain the gym."

We smiled. God was miraculously opening all the doors. All we had to do was step through those open doors. This was going to be easy.

"We want a long-term contract," I added. "Every weekend for one to two years."

The director's smile widened. "That is what we want too. Are you starting a martial arts class, yoga, or something? I am very interested in Eastern culture."

"No!" I blurted out. "We are going to start a church."

The smile on the director's face disappeared like it was vacuumed off with a 10,000 horsepower Dirt Devil vacuum. A menacing snarl appeared.

"What did you say you want to do with my gym?"

"We want to rent it for church services," I replied weakly. "We want a place where the community can come and worship God freely."

"There are enough churches here in this city. We do not need another one. What type of sect do you belong to?"

"Church is for the good of the community - much better than martial arts! We want people to know God personally."

The director got up and screamed at us. "You proselytes! The answer is NO! Get out of this place right now or I will throw you out! Call security!"

Credinescu grabbed my arm and we rushed out of the director's office. As we ran for the school's front door, we saw two uniformed guards approaching us from another hallway. The cleaning woman with her mop and bucket was not far behind them.

"Quick! Get out!" Credinescu wheezed.

I shot out of the building faster than a rabbit being chased by a pack of Communist wolves.

When we were a safe distance away and the hammering in our hearts had slowed down to the point where we could converse, Credinescu turned towards me.

"You shouldn't have mentioned church," he reprimanded.

"I thought he was friendly," I said, defensively. "He did mention he was interested in Eastern things and you can't look more Eastern than me!"

"Nobody will rent to us if we mention church!" Credinescu emphasized.

"Well, next time, let's just say we need the building for playing music," I replied. "If we leave out the Spirit, praise and worship *is* music."

"Yes! Let's do that."

"Anyway, let's not take this too hard. That building was way too old and horrid for us. It was good that the director said no to us. We want something more modern than that."

Credinescu echoed my self-justifications.

"Yes, who wants that ugly old building? Let's go for the modern instead!"

"And the acoustics in that gym would have been terrible! Four concrete walls will distort all our praise and worship."

"Yes, we want to sound good, not reverberating. It was good that he said no to us."

With this self-justification, we went in search for the next place.

❦

37. The Gilded Night Club

The next place was a nightclub called The Stone. It was situated just ten minutes away from the high school we had just given up on. The contrast between the two buildings was like night and day. While the school was a faded light green, The Stone was all glitzy and chrome. The windows at the school, though replaced, looked dingy. The wall-to-wall windows at The Stone scintillated like a myriad of stars.

"This is certainly different," I said, staring at the stony-glass structure.

"Very modern," Credinescu said. "Just what we want."

"Think of the acoustics - no distortions here!"

"That's good! Let's go in and find the manager."

We walked confidently into the lobby of the club. A perky blonde, oozing glitter, greeted us. I found myself unconsciously reaching for my Rayban's. We found out from the blonde that the manager had stepped out for a minute.

"You can wait for him right here," the girl indicated.

"Might as well," I said. "No point in leaving and then coming back later."

The blonde left us to shine elsewhere.

"This place looks impressive," Credinescu said, looking around the lobby. The polished tiles gleamed and shone. So did the wall to wall and ceiling mirrors.

"Mind you do not get sunburn," I joked.

"I am sure a lot of young people will come here if we can rent this place."

"Me too," I replied, looking at my reflection on the ceiling. "That is what we want – young people who do not go to church. We do not want anybody from any other church. There are thousands of people who do not go to church so we should be able to reach some."

"We will!"

After fifteen minutes, the manager appeared. He struck me as a tight man. He had on tight pants, a tight shirt, and tight shoes. The polyester gripped his figure so well that it revealed his thong underwear. The black shiny pointed polyester shoes complemented his burnished sartorial splendor.

"I understand from my secretary that you would like to rent this club," he said.

"Yes, we would," I affirmed.

"We would like to rent to you but unfortunately all our nights are fully booked," he began apologetically. "Mondays to Thursdays we have shows. Fridays and Saturdays we have disco. We are fully booked!"

"That's alright," I said. "We only want to rent this place on Sunday mornings!"

The polyester froze in shock.

"You want to rent this place on Sundays? But nobody goes to a disco on Sunday!"

"We just want a place to play music," I said, rehearsing our earlier conversation.

"Yes, we want to play music every Sunday morning," Credinescu chimed in.

"You have Sunday mornings free, right?" I asked.

The manager found his tongue. He looked concerned. "Yes, we definitely have the place free on Sunday mornings. We are only busy at nights. But I do not know why you would want it on Sundays. You know, maybe in a few months time, we might have Wednesday or Thursday nights free. We can rent those nights to you then."

"No, thanks," I said. "We just want Sunday mornings."

"Well, if that's what you want! We can give you a good deal for Sunday mornings as it is a dead time for us. We have a good sound system that you can use as well."

That sounded sweet to my ears. I looked at Credinescu and he looked back at me. Surely God was moving this time!

"Would you like to see the inside of our club?" the manager asked.

"Of course!" we concurred, enthusiastically.

We jumped up from our seats like beavers setting off for work and followed the manager to a thick metal door. He produced a key, unlocked the door and led us into the club.

My first impression of the club was that I had suddenly gone blind. It was like walking into black wool on a moonless night.

"I can't see anything," I said. "Can you please turn on the lights?"

The manager coughed politely. "The lights are on!"

"But I cannot see anything," I replied.

"Maybe your eyes have to adjust from the brightness outside," the manager suggested. "Give it a few minutes."

"My eyes are adjusting fine. I can only see where the light shines through the open door."

"Wait!" the manager said. "Let me see whether I can find some more lights."

He disappeared into the wooly black night.

"I can't see anything either," Credinescu whispered to me. "But we can always bring our own lighting here. A couple of 1000 watts flood lamps and this place would shine."

"You are a genius," I whispered back. "Of course we can light up this place."

At that precise moment, the whole back wall of the club came to life and glowed purple. As our eyes adjusted to the new purplish light, we marveled at the lush interior. It was setup like a stadium with the seats angling up and away towards the back wall. But in this club all the seats were red plush love seats which looked like mini-beds.

Directly in front of us was a huge empty expanse. I surmised that that was the dance space. But what caught our immediate attention was the gargantuan bar beneath the purplish lights - the whole back wall was filled with liquor displayed on multi-level glass shelves. I had never seen wall-to-wall alcohol before. It was amazing! I was still mesmerized by it when Credinescu murmured to me.

"The front here would be nice for altar calls."

"Do you see that thing at the back?" I asked. "There are enough bottles there to drown an Orca whale!"

Credinescu laughed himself silly. "I see what you mean. But look at the bright side. People can always reach for a drink when they find your sermons boring."

I gave him a withering stare. "I can just imagine what people will say when I invite them to church and they see enough alcohol there to float the Titanic. I don't think that makes a good start."

"Maybe we can get a big cloth and cover up the whole back wall," Credinescu suggested. He was full of brilliant ideas. "That way nobody will see the avalanche of alcohol."

"What happens if somebody came to us and asked us what we are trying to hide behind the big cloth?" I asked. "It is definitely not the Holy of Holies we are hiding back there!"

Credinescu changed the subject. "The seats look comfortable though. I have never seen such deep plush seats before in my entire life. You can sink into them."

"At least nobody will complain that the chairs are uncomfortable."

"So what do you think?" Credinescu asked.

"Well, with our own lights and a big enough cloth, we might make this work. As you mentioned, the space in front is huge."

"Yes, it is," Credinescu said, looking around and then up.

I followed suit and gasped.

"Do you see what I see?" I asked. "There are 2 golden cages right above us!"

Credinescu was too stunned to speak.

"I think those cages are for naked girls to dance in Saturday nights," I continued.

"Well, maybe you can preach from those cages Sunday mornings," Credinescu said.

"I can preach just about anywhere but I don't think I can preach from a golden cage. It just doesn't seem right."

I was beginning to wonder where the manager was when he materialized.

"What do you think?" he asked. "Nice place, isn't it? We can cram a thousand people here."

"We'll let you know," I said. "We have to discuss this some more between us."

"I can get my secretary to make up the contract right now. If you sign a two year lease, I can give you a very good price."

"Thanks for your offer, but we really have to think about it. We'll call you."

38. The Cinema and the Politician

"That didn't work out as well as I had expected it to," I said, as we exited The Stone.

"Yes, it would be hard to start a church with so much alcohol and suggestions of sex," Credinescu stated.

"Actually it's easy to attract people with alcohol and sex," I countered. "It's just that I don't think God would be very happy with that – huge doses of false anointing! By the way, I just had an idea. Why don't we go and see whether we can rent a cinema instead? There would be good acoustics there and definitely less gaudiness."

"Great idea! We can look up the local theater too. There is also a cultural house we can check out."

"What is a cultural house?"

"Something like a community center for students and other clubs."

"Let's visit all of them."

We talked about movies as we headed over to the local cinema. When we reached the cinema, we were informed that the only way to rent a cinema was to meet the Director of Entertainment for the city. He worked under some Ministry Office.

Before we checked with him, we decided to enquire at the other two cinemas, the theater, as well as the cultural house.

But the answers were all the same. Nothing could be done without the director's approval. Resigned to meeting the Director of Entertainment, we went over to his office.

The director's office was downtown, situated among magnificent buildings. However, the buildings, while magnificent, were in poor shape. But the stairs up to the director's office were pure marble and impeccable. A steady stream of humanity was moving up and down the marble staircase.

"This looks very high class," Credinescu remarked. "We are moving up on the social ladder."

"Maybe he will be more open to us," I said. "People up the social ladder sometimes are more open to new ideas. By the way, do you know who the director is?"

"I don't have a clue but we will find out soon."

When we reached the director's office, we were immediately assaulted with an onslaught of busyness: there were people babbling on phones, there were people on ladders hanging up signs and slogans, and there were people with cameras flashing away. Amid this hive, mobile phones rang, copiers copied, faxes faxed, and computers hummed. A cacophony of noise and excitement filled the atmosphere.

We inquired what was happening and was told that the director was running for Mayor of the city. The elections would be held in a few days time.

"Is the director in?" I asked the secretary. "We just need a few minutes of his time."

The secretary, a pretty brunette, asked us to wait while she checked.

We were soon ushered into the inner chambers of the director's office. After hearty handshakes, we sat down facing the director.

He was a big man, splendidly dressed, with an intelligent face. He was most cordial in his insistence that we be served drinks and cookies.

"How can I help you?" he boomed hospitably. His voice sounded like a foghorn.

"We would like to rent one of the city cinemas on Sunday mornings," I began. "We were told to see you for this."

"For what purpose? Why do you want to rent a cinema?"

"We want to start a church," I blurted. "Something for the community."

I waited for the rejection.

"That is a great idea," the director said unexpectedly. "We need more help in the community. I am running for mayor in this city and I am aware of how much help is needed. Our teenagers are running wild, drugs are rampant, and crime is up. We are short of funds as usual; so a new church helping out in the community is great. Let me speak to some people first and then get back to you. I promise you a space. I am very sorry that I cannot spend more time with you today, but I have a very tight schedule. Come back in a few days, after the election is over, and we will see what we can do for you. We may even be able to give you the space rent-free."

I glanced at Credinescu. Surely *this time* it was God moving.

"We hope you will win the mayoral seat," Credinescu said.

"Thank-you!" the director boomed again. "Don't forget to vote!"

He shook our hands heartily again as we left.

. . . .

Exactly five days later, we were climbing up the same marble steps to the director's office.

"Hey, there's nobody here today!" I remarked. "Very different environment than the bustle and noise from a few days earlier."

"Pity that he did not win the mayor's post," Credinescu said. "But he should have more time for us today."

"Yes, he seemed really affable. It would have been nice to have a mayor supporting our effort. Still, he did promise to give us a place – probably not for free now as he did not win the election."

"A place is better than no place," Credinescu postulated.

"You are absolutely right," I said.

We reached the doors to the office, knocked, and entered. The banners, phones, reporters, and machines were all gone now. Only the brunette secretary was left. She was perusing the newspapers as we entered. She eyed us antagonistically.

"Good morning!" I said. "We came back to see the director as requested."

The secretary put down the newspapers. "Exactly who are you and what do you want?"

We smiled broadly. "Surely you remember us? We were here a few days ago. The director asked us to come back. We want to rent a cinema from him."

"I don't remember you two at all," the secretary stalled.

"We remember you," Credinescu chipped in. "Why don't you call the director? He will remember us."

The secretary looked at Credinescu condescendingly before picking up the phone. Grumbling was heard from the other side. After a few seconds, she hung up the phone.

"I spoke to the director. He has no idea who you are. He is a very busy man and is not meeting anybody for the rest of the month. After that, he is going away for another few months. Why don't you come back in six months time? Maybe you can catch him then."

"But... but he promised to see us," I stammered.

The brunette got exasperated. "Didn't you hear me? He does not remember you at all and I am sure he did not make any promises to you. It is our lunch time now and we are closed. Would you two mind waiting outside?"

"That's all right," I said. "We are going. We know when we are not wanted."

"Politicians and their promises!" Credinescu spit out.

I grabbed him by his shoulder and pulled him out.

"Nothing we can do," I said. "But he could have told us 'no' a few days ago instead of giving us false hope."

"Politicians!" Credinescu said heatedly "They're the same everywhere. They promise everything before the elections and then do nothing afterwards. They promise us roads and give us holes. They promise us a better life and they are the only ones to see this better life. They get fat from lying and cheating."

I tried to steer Credinescu away from politics.

"Well, there goes the opportunity to rent any cinemas. Those were all the public places available…including the high school and club. Are there any private kindergartens around? Maybe we can rent one?"

Credinescu looked at me like I had gone mad. "Have you seen the chairs they use in kindergartens? They are tiny! We can't sit like midgets for church!"

"How about private hotels?" I asked. "They might have a conference room free."

"There are no private hotels here. You forget that Romania was a closed country. The only hotels ever built were built by the Communists and they were heavily bugged. I don't think they will welcome a church."

"I'm running out of ideas. Do you have any suggestions?"

"Let me think."

After some thinking, his eyes suddenly lit up.

"There is a grade school left. We can try that place."

"Yes," I said, dejectedly. "What's the harm? The worst thing that can happen is that we will be rejected again."

"Do you remember telling me that I could become the insect that everybody steps on? Well, ever since we started to look for a place, I have been rejected by more people than I can even remember. I have never felt so rejected in my entire life!"

"Welcome to the reject club!" I replied. "This is only the beginning."

39. The Grade School

The grade school was the poster child for all things Communist. It was an enormous, grey slab of concrete sitting on several acres of weeds close to an abandoned industrial site. The building itself was punctuated by holes and covered with broken green glass. Through unhinged doors we caught glimpses of dripping and broken pipes, and holes in the ground where toilets once were as we made our way to the director's office.

The director, who looked older than Moses, had a long, slender figure with strings of shiny white hair brushed back from his forehead. He had a toothless face and his hand gestures were deliberately slow. There was a generous dose of senility mixed with a liberal pinch of antiquity in his behavior.

"Teenagers nowadays are not what they used to be," the director began.

We nodded our heads.

"We were never bad growing up during Communist times," the director continued. "Those were the good old days. Everybody had jobs and houses then. We produced everything we needed without having to import anything. And our worst behavior in school was to tease our classmates. We produced the best tractors, then too! Maybe I am getting too old for this job as I cannot understand teenagers at all. I do not know why they behave so disrespectfully and rude to their parents and teachers. Today we caught one boy beating up his teacher. In my time, we would have never dared to do such a thing. And yes, our tractors were the best in the world. They never failed us – no, not even once."

I tried my best to follow him but the 'Little Tractor That Could' kept punctuating my thoughts. I wanted to laugh but instead I commiserated with the director in his office.

When the condolences for the death of 'respect' were over, the director suddenly woke up from his reverie.

"What can I do for you?" he asked.

"We were wondering if you have a gymnasium we could rent every weekend?" I asked, sheepishly.

"Yes we have a small gym," he replied. "What would you like to do there?"

"We believe we can help teenagers learn to respect themselves and others. We want to teach and help them learn some useful, positive things. To that end, we would like to start a church."

The director looked at me ruefully, his old fossilized body bent over painfully. "I like the idea of teaching something useful to the youth but it is illegal to rent out public property for private use. I have to say No to you. Why don't you go and rent a private cinema or club?"

Credinescu and I looked at each other in dismay.

"We tried that already, but it did not work out," Credinescu said. "Back in the village of Santandrei where I grew up, we could always rent public buildings for events."

The director suddenly bounded up straight in his chair. "Santandrei? Did you say Santandrei? I was born in Santandrei!"

With that single word, Credinescu and the director exchanged a rapid-fire discussion which ended with the discovery that they had many mutual friends and could even be long-lost relatives.

"Of course, we can rent the gym to you," the director said warmly, exuding nepotism. "We do not have to let the government know that I am renting the building to you. In return, maybe you can help us upgrade our ancient school. We do not have any computers in this school. Maybe you can help us build a computer lab?"

"I agree," I said. "We can buy computers for the school in exchange for the space. By the way, can we see the gym please?"

"Of course," the director replied. "Let me take you there myself. Now, where are my keys?"

He got up from his chair, his bones creaking louder than the chair. I wanted to sign the contract right then and there - afraid he might die before we had a chance to seal the heavily 'nepotisized' agreement.

Finally, he found his keys. "Follow me."

We fell in behind the director, following his footsteps.

"It's great that you two come from the same region of the country," I whispered to Credinescu. "Funny how he did a complete turnaround after that!"

"Yes, blood relations are very strong in this country," Credinescu whispered back. "We seem to be going around in circles. Do you think we are lost?"

"He's the director of the school," I murmured back. "He cannot be lost in his own school."

"Did you count the number of doors, staircases, short and long corridors that we passed? I counted ten doors, four staircases, eight short corridors, and three long ones already."

"And all the doors are solid steel," I added. "They are guarding this gym better than the gold in Fort Knox. It must really be something."

Just as I thought that we were never going to arrive, the director stopped at a thick metal door.

"This is the last door," he said. "We had to walk all that way because the gym is actually outside the school. This is the connecting door."

He unlocked the door, threw it open, and we stepped into the gym.

Credinescu and I gasped silently at the interior of the gym. The floors were a muddy brown; the solid concrete walls were plastered half-green and half-mottled-white. Large chunks of plaster were missing everywhere. This was probably caused by eons of basketball and football. There were also some marks on the walls that suspiciously resembled blood. As we watched, a chunk of white fell to the floor with a quiet sigh to reveal a moldy green underneath. Above the walls were arrays of dirty green and brown windows. They had holes the size of watermelons in them. Nevertheless, every window was protected by crisscrossed steel rebars.

"What do you think?" the director said, as he flipped on the lights. "This is our gym."

Unfortunately the lights did not come on. He spent the next minute toggling the buttons up and down. In the end, he succeeded in pulling the whole wall plate, together with the switch, out of the wall and exposing the bare wires behind it.

The director stared absent-mindedly at the switching apparatus in his hand. He had no clue that his school was caving in on him.

"This will be repaired by the time you start," he said optimistically.

Credinescu and I looked at each other again. We had seen reasonably good high school gyms, nice bars, great cinemas, theaters, and cultural centers, but had been rejected or turned off by all. This was the sole remaining structure that was open to us, but it was also the ugliest! On the bright side though, it was still standing.

"We'll take it," I said. "This will be a great place for us to start."

Little did we know we would end up staying in that gym for the next seven years. And during those years, we would buy enough computers for the school to furnish all its computer labs, as well as computers for all the administrative staff. We even bought a laptop for the director. When winter came, he finally learned how to turn it on. I guessed he liked the hot air blowing out the back of his laptop.

40. Is that a Patient on the Road?

It had now been some time since my first car was stolen. I missed the excitement of driving. I also missed the sensation of accomplishing fewer things faster with a car. It was impossible to replicate that feeling by walking all over the city.

I heard of a used car dealer located outside the city and decided to visit it one late afternoon. The lot was full of very nice cars and I was impressed. After some time, a salesman wearing an Italian suit, but made-in-Romania, walked up.

"Where do you get all these high-end cars?" I asked curiously.

"We import them from Germany," he replied. "Individuals, companies, rental agencies – we buy from them and bring the cars back here to Romania."

"Your prices seem a little high," I postulated.

"We have good prices. If you want cheap prices, go and buy from a person advertising in the local newspaper. The car will probably be stolen from Italy with a set of false papers. You buy at your own risk. We operate legally."

"I was looking at this car here…" I began, but was interrupted by another customer.

"Do you have the car ready for me?" the other customer inquired.

"Excuse me," the salesman said. "I have to take care of this customer. He has special-ordered a Mercedes with extra wide seats to accommodate his size. In the meantime, feel free to look around our inventory of cars."

But I was curious about those extra wide seats and followed the salesman to a silver Mercedes that still bore a sales tag of US$55,000. After some discussion, the new customer handed a small suitcase over to the salesman. Without a trace of discomfort, the salesman flipped open the bag. I choked when I saw the bundles of cash inside. It reminded me of drug deals I had seen on television. I had never seen so much cash being used so freely.

The salesman saw my astonishment.

"We only accept cash here."

"Don't you accept credit?" I asked. "In America, we finance our cars with credit."

"No, no credit. Only cash!"

Out of curiosity, I followed the salesman and his client into his office. I sat as quiet as a cactus as the salesman and his colleagues counted the $55,000. Then, after a few signatures, the client left in a screech of rubber.

"That was a lot of money to count," I said.

"That was nothing," the salesman replied. "We have about half a million dollars in our safe which we will deposit in the bank today."

"Isn't it dangerous to carry that much cash?"

The salesman looked at his colleagues. They nodded their heads unanimously.

"Let me show you something," he said. He peeled back his jacket so I could see the gun in its holster clearly. At the same time, his colleagues peeled back their jackets and showed me their guns. There were enough guns in the showroom to conquer neighboring Serbia.

"As you can see we feel very safe," he said. "Now which car were you looking at?"

"I was looking at that black car," I gulped.

"Nice car. One previous owner from Germany. Come back with the cash and it's yours."

"I don't feel comfortable carrying that much cash."

"You worry too much. Carrying cash is perfectly safe."

"I will think about it," I replied.

. . . .

It took me a few days to think about it. I finally decided to go ahead and buy the car. But I still had to transfer the money over from New York. Strugurescu, my now in-the-army friend, offered to help.

"I have a bank account which you can use," he said. "I never use the account anyway."

"Since I cannot open an account here in this country, I will use your account," I replied. "It's for one transaction only."

"When the transfer is complete, we will go to the bank and withdraw it together. Don't worry; I am not going to cheat you."

"I am low on trust," I confided. "But I trust you. The transfer will take a maximum of three days."

Exactly three days later, the money for the car arrived. I called Strugurescu and we agreed to meet at the bank. Black Bear, my landlord, who was collecting rent money that morning, proposed that I ride with him to the bank.

"I appreciate you giving me a lift," I said.

"No problem," Black Bear growled. "Why do you need to go to the bank?"

I explained that Strugurescu was helping me with a big transfer.

Black Bear reacted unexpectedly. "Are you sure you can trust him?"

"You introduced him to me, remember?" I said. "Are you trying to tell me now that he cannot be trusted? I have been out many times with him. I even met his family."

"That's nothing," Black Bear snarled. "People here would willingly sell their families for cash. Mothers are cheap, wives even cheaper. The sum you are transferring in - that's equivalent to ten to twenty years of his salary! Are you sure Strugurescu will be at the bank waiting for you?"

"I trust Strugurescu," I said, my voice full of doubt. "He will be at the bank."

. . . .

But he was not!

I rushed into the bank.

"Strugurescu has withdrawn the full sum," a cashier told me. "He left five minutes ago."

I rushed out again. Black Bear was waiting for me.

"He left with all the money!" I said. "He came to the bank early and withdrew the money. I don't know where he is. I can't see him anywhere."

"I told you so!" Black Bear thundered. "He is not to be trusted!"

"That's incredible!"

"Let me drive you up and down this street. Maybe we can catch Strugurescu somewhere."

"That's useless," I countered. "We will never be able to spot him in this crowd. He might have taken a taxi. Quick! Drive me to his apartment. If we are fast, we can lie in wait for him."

Black Bear licked his jaws. "Good idea!"

He shot out of the parking lot and quickly reached Strugurescu's place.

"How do we know that he had not arrived yet?" Black Bear asked.

"I'll go up to his apartment and check," I said, jumping out of the car.

I crept up the three flights of stairs to Strugurescu's apartment. With my heart hammering, I reached his door and stealthily put my ear against it. Through the wood, I could clearly hear a woman and a child talking and playing. I stayed for a minute to confirm that Strugurescu was not at home. When I was sure, I crept down the stairs again. This creeping around did not agree with me.

"I don't like this," I said. "But I'm sure that he's not home yet."

"I can call some of my friends here to deal with him," Black Bear suggested.

Visions of the wild, wild, west lawyer and his idea to half-kill people flashed before my eyes.

"We don't need that," I said quickly. "Strugurescu only had a five minute head start. He will be here soon, I hope. Let's hide behind the entrance door so we can surprise him when he comes."

My heart hammered painfully in my chest as we waited. All was quiet. Then through a slit in the door, we saw Strugurescu, clutching a small satchel, hurrying up the path directly towards us. I pounced on him as he entered.

"Where were you?" I asked. "I went to the bank and you were gone!"

Strugurescu winced. His guilty face said it all. "I waited for you but you did not come."

"You are lying!" Black Bear thundered. "We were there on time but you had already left."

"Do you have my money?" I asked.

"Yes, I was going to give it to you," Strugurescu said, handing over the money. "I was just going to call you to tell you I have the money. I am bringing it home for safekeeping."

It was the lamest excuse I had ever heard.

"Let's go," Black Bear ordered.

I needed no further encouragement. We left Strugurescu on the stairs. Once back in the car, I began to breathe again.

"Do you think that Strugurescu could have been telling the truth?" I asked. "Maybe I did just miss him at the bank."

Black Bear eyed me darkly. "Never trust anybody in this country. Strugurescu would have sold his wife and son for a fraction of that money."

I sighed, knowing that he was probably right. Once again, I had almost been cheated for trusting a person. I felt that I was under a 'dumbness' curse. Or maybe I had inadvertently taken some 'dumb' pills. The effect was the same - I felt dumb.

Black Bear dropped me off at the street corner where the car dealership was. With money in hand, I walked in.

. . . .

"You are back," the affable salesman said.

"Yes, I have decided to take the car," I said. "I almost did not make it. I had some problems at the bank."

The salesman did not wait for my explanation but jumped to his own conclusion. "There are people lurking outside banks waiting for customers loaded with cash to come out. Just last year, one of our clients lost $50,000 that way."

I humored him. He did not need to know about the dumbness curse. "How would the thieves lurking outside know who has money? I mean, almost everyone carries a bag here."

"They have an accomplice working in the bank. The accomplice alert the thieves who to look for. Our client was marked before he exited the bank. He was knocked on the head and all his money was stolen!"

"I never knew buying a car could be so dangerous," I said, ambiguously.

"It is not when you have a gun," the salesman repeated, patting his breast. "Shall we go for a test drive?"

I jumped into the car with the salesman. We whizzed out of the dealership. However, it didn't last long. We were stopped by a mob standing in the middle of the street.

"What's happening?" I cried, expecting a stick-up.

"Seems like a disturbance of some type," the salesman replied. "Don't worry; it has nothing to do with us."

I relaxed, and then craned my neck to look over the sea of people. The salesman got out.

"Let's go and see what this is about!" he shouted to me.

"But you are parked in the middle of the street!" I began.

"That's alright. Nobody would dare touch the car."

"If you say so," I replied.

We pushed our way into the crowd. People were gesticulating and screaming loudly.

"What's happening?" I asked again, as we squeezed through.

"I see a man lying in the middle of the street," the salesman replied. He was talking rapidly to some people and gathering information.

"Is he drunk?" I asked. "Drunks do fall over in the street."

"No, from what I am able to gather, an ambulance dumped him on the street!"

"Why would an ambulance dump a patient on the road?"

"It seems like he suffered a seizure," the salesman explained. "Somebody called an ambulance which took him to a hospital. That hospital was full and refused to admit him. The ambulance driver drove him to another hospital where the nurses asked him whether he had insurance. He didn't, so they refused to admit him, also. By now, the ambulance driver was hopping mad. He didn't want to drive all over the city looking for a hospital. The third and last hospital wanted a bribe. The patient had no money so they refused to inter him too. The ambulance driver was so mad with everybody that he drove here - right in the middle of the city - and dumped his patient in the middle of this busy street. Now all the traffic is blocked and the people are incensed that a sick man is lying in the middle of the street!"

"Are they angry because of the way the man was treated by the hospitals and the ambulance driver or are they angry because the man is blocking traffic?" I asked incredulously.

"Probably both," the salesman said, shaking his head and fingering his gun holster. "The way the hospitals treat the public is outrageous. If I could I would kill them all. Some people are alive in this country only because it is illegal to kill them! This man's only fault is that he is poor!"

"Look!" I addressed the vigilante salesman. "Why don't you take the man to the hospital? The hospital staff may let the man in if they see your car."

The salesman stared at me. "I cannot, this is not my car. And it is not your car either. Not yet anyway."

"But you just told me that the man's fault is that he's poor. We can help him."

"I cannot. I would lose my job."

"If we don't help him, then who is going to help him?"

"Somebody else. I can't take this man to the hospital. I can only transport potential buyers in this car."

I couldn't persuade the salesman to make an exception. As we left the man in the middle of the road, I wondered about my own priorities. But I was exhausted from chasing after Strugurescu all morning and did not press the issue.

As we finished signing all of the paperwork for the sale of the car that afternoon, I could not help feeling the injustice of it all. Also, I could not stop wondering what had happened to the man who was left out on the street to die because he was poor.

41. Immigration I

At about that time too, I had to renew my visa in order to continue staying on in Romania. I discovered where the immigration office was and drove there.

"Where is the line for renewing visas?" I asked the police guards at the front of the immigration office.

One of them looked at me, spit on the floor, and pointed to a chaotic line of about five hundred sweaty people - all crushed together trying to get a foot into the one and only door of the Immigration and Passport Office.

I looked at the heaving undulating mass and gritted my teeth. I didn't have a choice. It was do it or leave the country. I inhaled deeply and plunged myself into the swell. Immediately I was sucked into the madness: the madness of Romania's immigration offices!

"Stop pushing!" a man yelled in my face, after an hour of pushing and shoving.

"I am not pushing," I shot back. "It's those people at the back. Ask them not to push!"

He yelled and cursed the people at the back of the line.

A wave of cacophonic curses swept back and drowned him in insults. His face turned a putrid shade of purple. I tried to distance myself from him but was unable to move. In fact, nobody had advanced at all for at least an hour! We just eddied back and forth, stuck in the same position.

Somebody stomped on the back of my foot and my shoe came loose. I elbowed the people around me to rescue my shoe - and just in time! As I slipped my shoe back on, the crowd surged forward two feet before rippling back a foot. A sense of renewed hope went through the crowd. The line had finally moved!

"Why is it going so slowly?" I asked the man in front of me.

"Those Communist workers inside don't work!" the man said bitterly.

"They are drinking coffee and reading newspapers while we die here!" a woman joined in. "Curse them and their families!"

"Nobody cares about us!" another man rejoined. "Fire them all!"

"It is always like this!" the first man replied. "Unless you pay them some money they don't care about helping you. If you pay them, you can get your passport in one day!"

"I'm not going to bribe anyone anymore," I replied.

"Blasted Communist workers!" the woman screamed. "I've been here since 5:00 am! Since Ceausescu died nothing has changed. The same blasted Communist attitudes!"

Three hours and six feet of progress later, the crowd grew incensed. The anger boiled over when some latecomers were ushered in by the police ahead of the line.

"Bribery!" a man shouted, raising his fists in fury.

"Kick them out!" the woman by my side screamed.

That proved too much for the police. They walked over to the line and stared at the people condescendingly. A hush fell over the undulating, pulsating mass.

"Who said that?" a policeman shouted.

There was deathly silence. The faces surrounding me looked down sullenly.

"What are you doing here?" a policeman bawled at me.

"Who, me?" I asked in surprise.

"Yes, what are you doing in this line?"

"I'm here to renew my visa. One of your colleagues told me to join the line this morning."

"I don't know why he would say that. There is a separate line for foreigners. This line is only for citizens. Get out and go line up over there."

"Have a good day!" I whispered to my fellow sufferers as I left the line. They stared at me enviously as I left to join the foreigners' line.

That line was much shorter. Only about twenty people!

"Did you come from the other line?" a sympathetic woman asked.

"Yes, I waited for more than four hours before they told me I was in the wrong line. Thank God this line is shorter."

"You may not be so thankful," the woman warned. "This line is shorter but there is only one person serving all of us and he has just left for lunch and will not be back until 2:00 pm. The other line for citizens is longer but they have several people serving them."

"They're not moving either," I said. "Either way we will be here until tomorrow!"

"They close at four," the woman replied.

"I think we should all pray," I muttered.

The prayer must have worked. At 3:45 pm, I found myself at the front of the line staring at a blank beige wooden door.

I knocked on the door politely.

Suddenly, without warning, a cutout in the wooden door jerked open and a man's face peered through. I stared at the face, as the door itself remained closed.

"What do you want?" the face barked.

"I came here to renew my visa."

"Today is only for passport pickups. Come back tomorrow for visa renewals!"

And with that the cutout door was slammed in my face.

42. Immigration II

Somebody once told me that living in Romania is a full time job. I tend to agree. I can spend a lot of time accomplishing absolutely nothing. I resolved to change that.

Next morning, I woke up at five and dashed to the Immigration Office. To my utter surprise, the same 500 people were already there shoving, jostling, and pushing their way toward the sole entrance door. But this time I knew better than to enter that line.

I went to the beige door instead. I smiled smugly when I discovered I was the first person in line. Persistence had paid off. I spent the next few hours examining the door. The wooden door was like any other door except that a big panel had been roughly cut out with a handsaw. It was akin to the lid of a coffin whereby a portion could swing up for viewing the departed loved one. Only difference was that there was no love here.

At nine sharp, the panel swung back.

"What do you want?" a voice demanded. I looked at the face. It was a different face than the one yesterday but the same insolence.

"I came to renew my visa."

"Give me your passport."

I gave the face in the door my passport.

"Wait here!"

He slammed the cutout door in my face. Second time, I counted mentally. After half an hour he returned with a sheave of papers, my passport included, in his hand which he tossed in my direction.

"Make a copy of your passport, fill up all of these forms and then come back."

The cutout panel slammed in my face. Third time! I didn't bat an eyelid. I perused the forms carefully. I saw that I had to pay at five different institutions varying amounts of fees. The highest amount was at a state bank and the lowest was at the post office for a 2 cent stamp. Each of those institutions would require a minimum of one day standing in line.

As predicted, it took the next five days for me to collect the various receipts from the five different institutions. Finally, with all the necessary forms filled and with receipts in hand, I headed back to Immigration.

This time, I stared without emotion at the same 500 people elbowing and shouldering one another as they fought for their lives to enter the office. I was too stuck in my own misery to notice their misery.

As before, the door slammed in my face a few times before a miracle happened. A woman unlocked the door and asked me to step in! I was overwhelmed with gratitude. I handed her the documents as we sat down on benches that suspiciously resembled those at school canteens. She examined the forms and receipts carefully.

"You seem to have all the forms filled out correctly," she began. "And I see that you paid all the required monies."

I smiled. ·

"But one of your receipts is wrong."

I stopped smiling.

"Which one?" I gulped. "I followed everything to the letter."

"That 2 cent stamp!'

"What's wrong with it?" I inquired. "It says 2 cents on it."

"That's a wrong 2 cent stamp. You bought a postage stamp. We require a special 2 cent stamp made specifically for these types of applications."

"How am I supposed to know that there are different types of 2 cent stamps?" I cried.

"You should have asked the people at the post office."

"I did. They sold me this one!"

"Well, it's wrong. Go and get a correct one."

As I walked out dejectedly, the beige door slammed behind me purposefully.

....

Unfortunately, a general strike took place after that which shut down the post office for a week. At the first opportunity possible, I bought a correct 2 cent stamp, waited the obligatory few hours at the beige door before confronting the same woman from before.

"I have the correct stamp this time," I said smugly. "Look at the distinctive symbol at the corner of this stamp. This is definitely not a postage stamp!"

She looked at me in exasperation.

"The symbol is right but the denomination is wrong. We need a 5 cent stamp. You have a 2 cent one here."

"But you told me that I needed a 2 cent stamp last time!"

"The immigration law has changed since then. It is now 5 cents."

I tried to obtain a grandfather clause. "When I obtained the forms, it was still 2 cents. You told me that yourself. Can't you apply that retrospectively in my case?"

"It was only valid then, not now. You should have submitted in your papers earlier."

She obviously did not like grandfathers so I tried logic.

"There was a strike. Then it took me a whole day at the post office just to buy that special 2 cent stamp. This whole process of buying one stamp has taken me more than 2 weeks. Can you please make an exception?"

"We still need a 5 cent stamp!"

"Please don't ask me to go to the post office again and then come back here. By then, the law may have changed! The difference is only three cents but it takes a long time to get it. Look, I'll give you a dollar instead for the 5 cent stamp."

"We don't sell 5 cent stamps here. You will have to come back after you obtain that stamp."

She showed me out. My shoulders slumped to the floor as the beige door slammed behind me again. How many times was that? I had lost count.

ॐॐ

43. Immigration III

About a month after I had correctly filed all the required documents and receipts, I received a call from the Immigration Office.

"About time I got approved," I muttered to myself. "This process to renew a visa is pure madness."

When I reached the Immigration and Passport office, I stared indifferently at 500 people, who looked exactly like the 500 people I had left a month ago, still crammed and wedged in the same spot. My heart had hardened considerably since this process began. I made my way to the familiar beige door, knocked and asked for my visa.

"Wait!" a voice said, and slammed the door in my face. I did not flinch a muscle.

About an hour later, I was asked to enter.

"What do you want?" a man asked.

"I came to get my visa approval," I said, showing him my passport.

He glanced at it perfunctorily.

"We have a problem," the man said.

"What kind of problem?"

"You will have to see the director for that."

"What for?" I asked.

The man did not answer, but led me down a long hall to another office where I was politely asked to sit down facing the Director of Immigration.

"What's the matter?" I asked. "I just came to collect my visa approval today."

Facing me, the stern man in a stiff uniform did not answer my question.

"Let me see your passport," he said.

I handed him my passport. He flipped through the worn pages.

"You have overstayed your visa by two days."

"I don't understand," I said, puzzled.

"Your visa has expired and you are still in this country. That means you have broken the law."

"No, I did not! I filed all the papers to renew my visa more than a month ago. In fact, I expected the approval some time ago. I hope you can stamp my passport with the new visa today. Wasn't that why I was called in today?"

"That was not the reason we called you in. We have a record of all the foreigners here in this city and we know that your visa has expired. But we have no record of you filing any renewal papers."

I could not believe my ears. "I was here – several times. You can ask your colleagues. They should recognize me."

"Before we called you in, we checked for those papers and did not find any. There is no record of it anywhere. You are now illegal in this country and must pay a fine."

"I filed those papers!" I cried. "There was a man who gave me some wrong information, then there was a woman who gave me some other information, then..."

"You can say what you want. We did not receive your file."

"Why don't you call your colleagues? They would recognize me!"

"It does not matter. The papers which you claim you filed are not here. You must pay the fine or we will send you to prison!"

I didn't know whether he was telling the truth or not but I did not want to end up in prison.

"How much is the fine?" I asked.

"Considering that you have overstayed your visa by only 2 days, we will charge you the minimum fine of US$350."

"$350?" I gasped.

"Yes, that is the minimum. We could fine you up to US$2,000 for overstaying. So consider this as a goodwill gesture. You have to pay this fine today. Tomorrow the fine will be US$700."

I paid the fine.

The director stated matter-of-factly. "This fine will extend your visa for one week. In this time, if you wish to stay, you have to file all the required papers. Make sure that you fulfill all the requirements to the letter. Do not make the mistake of overstaying again! Next time, we will not be so accommodating."

I didn't know whether to laugh or to cry.

☙❧

44. Legalism 101

In the meantime, Credinescu had become my good friend. Through his connections, I was invited to preach at a small church in a small village. The village was so remote that news of who I was had not reached them yet. It was also my first encounter with legalism and it started with Pastor Smeurescu.

We met Smeurescu outside the church building. The building was dressed in a shiny white coat of fresh acrylic paint and Smeurescu was dressed in a shiny black coat of old polyester.

Mr. Smeurescu swallowed hard and painfully when he saw us. He extended out his hand reluctantly.

"Peace!" he mouthed. He looked far from peaceful.

"Peace!" I replied back. I wondered whether his underwear was too tight for him.

"Peace!" Credinescu said, his face shining from excitement.

"How was your trip here?" Mr. Smeurescu inquired. His tone was as cold as an embalmer.

"No problems," I said. "Thanks for inviting us here today."

Mr. Smeurescu addressed Credinescu. "Can I have a word with you?"

They walked ahead conversing in low tones. After a minute or two, Smeurescu disappeared into the church building.

"What's bothering him?" I asked. "He doesn't seem too pleased to see us. And what were you two whispering about back there?"

Credinescu gave me a half-hearted smile. "Don't worry! Everything is fine. Let's go in."

We walked into the sanctuary. It was packed ten people to every five chairs. Every eye turned towards us as we entered. I was probably the first foreigner they had ever seen in their lives. I smiled benevolently and tried to be nonchalant.

"I'm going to sit here," I said, indicating a half empty spot at the back of the church.

Credinescu looked around and seeing no other empty seats squeezed in beside me. We had hardly settled down when Mr. Smeurescu rushed over.

"Why are you sitting here?" Mr. Smeurescu asked, in great agitation.

"I hope you do not mind," I said. "This was the only empty spot we found."

"You are sitting in the wrong side of the church!"

"I didn't know there was a right side and a wrong side."

"This side of the church is only for women. It is a sin to sit here with the women."

"Shall we stand then?" I asked.

"No! It is a sin to stand when everybody else is sitting."

"Tell us where to sit and we will sit there," I said. "The other side is full and we don't want to sit in some men's lap."

"We are bringing in some more chairs from the kitchen," Mr. Smeurescu said. "You can sit up front then."

"Anything else that I should know about?" I whispered to him.

Mr. Smeurescu's anguished face took on a tormented hue.

"Your watch!" he gasped.

I looked at my watch. It looked fine.

"What's wrong with my watch?" I asked curiously.

"Wearing a watch is a sin here," Mr. Smeurescu breathed. "It is a sign of pride!"

"I can take off my watch," I said. I was beginning to understand what had caused his anguish and lack-of-peace from before.

"Your tie and jacket too!" Mr. Smeurescu said his face gnawed with pain. "It is also a sign of pride."

"But I was told by somebody here in Romania to never preach without wearing a jacket and tie."

"Not here. Here it is a sin!"

"I can take off my jacket and tie easily."

"Do it!" Mr. Smeurescu whispered in my ear. "I may be the pastor here, but the elders make the rules. I do not care about such things but I have to follow the rules too. They are observing me closely. I may lose my job if I do not obey them!"

"Don't worry!" I whispered back. "I am here to help you."

Mr.Smeurescu sighed heavily.

"I just want to preach the gospel of Jesus Christ. That is what I wanted to do my whole life. But I have to follow the rules!"

I was saved from answering by the noisy arrival of more chairs.

"Let's go up front and praise God," Mr. Smeurescu said.

"Let's go," I said to Credinescu.

Mr. Smeurescu put out a hand and physically restrained Credinescu. "No, he has to stay here with the others."

"Why?" I asked in astonishment. "He's with me!"

"The elders and deacons do not want a non-ordained person to sit up front."

"That's OK," Credinescu interrupted. "I don't mind sitting back here."

Stripped from my friend, my watch, my tie, and my jacket, I followed Mr. Smeurescu up front to deliver a message on freedom from bondage in Christ.

45. Legalism 102

After the church program, Mr. Smeurescu invited us over to his house for lunch. We discovered that his wife had prepared a banquet fit for a host of armies in her tiny living room. Food was piled high on the sideboards, the shelves, and even the beds. There were more pots of simmering soups and fried meats in the kitchen.

Credinescu and I settled down amidst these bounties.

"How do you like our church?" Mr. Smeurescu asked.

"It was interesting," I replied, choosing my words carefully.

"The rules that we have may seem strange to you but all of them were imposed by the deacons and other leaders before I became the pastor here. I have been here for five years now and try as I could, nothing has changed."

"Ah, so you are deacon possessed," I muttered softly.

"What's that you said?"

"Nothing!"

"I went to Bible College where I had a great time. My colleagues and I were so much on fire. We just wanted to go out and share the Word of God with everybody. But after graduation I got married, then the kids came, and I needed a job desperately. My professors helped me find this church and I have been here ever since."

"I understand," I said. "So you just towed the line. That happens to a lot of pastors."

"Yes, but I feel so helpless. I thought I could make some changes here but the people are so resistant, downright militant sometimes! All they care about is their image and maintaining that appearance at all costs."

"You mean about the legalism?"

"Yes, that's what I meant. Do you know that they judge the spirituality of the women in the church by how big their head coverings are? The bigger the more spiritual!"

"So that explains all the head scarves I saw in the church. But I know women in certain parts of this world who cover up their entire body. Even their eyes are covered. If what you say is true then these covered-up women must be the holiest people on earth. But what about the youth? Do they follow the rules too?"

Mr. Smeurescu's face pained significantly. "We have lost all but a few of our youth. They get judged on everything. After a while, the youth just disappeared. I often see them in the clubs instead. Their parents are desperate, but there is nothing I can do about that."

"Talking about deacons, as we left the church, I saw that deacon who was handing out the elements for communion earlier drunk outside the church building. I have met a lot of drunks in my life to recognize the symptoms. Does that deacon drink secretly outside the church?"

"No, he doesn't," Mr. Smeurescu said. His eyes clouded over. "He drinks in the church!"

"I don't understand," I said.

"In our church, one of the rules is that none of the communion elements be wasted. So all the leftover wine and bread must be drunk and eaten."

"I understand. He has to drink all the leftover wine!'

"Exactly! And there was plenty left over today."

"On that note, I noticed that only a few women actually partook communion. The vast majority just sat there. Why is that so?"

"Well, women who are menstruating cannot take communion. It is in Leviticus."

"You don't mean to tell me that over 90% of your women are menstruating at the same time? The PMS time must be crazy!"

Mr. Smeurescu seemed genuinely shocked. "No, I don't mean that at all. A few of them may be having their period but most of them feel that they are not pure or good enough to drink and eat with the Lord."

"None of us are," I replied. "It is through what Jesus has done for us that makes us able to sit down with Him."

"You don't have to tell me, but that's not what these people are taught."

"Why don't you teach them the truth?"

"I can't," Mr. Smeurescu said. "I need this job."

"These fried pork cutlets are really good," Credinescu mouthed. "Are you two going to eat or do I have to eat everything myself?"

இ~இ

46. Legalism 103

The rehearsal place for my newly-formed Praise and Worship team was in the school gym. The team was a motley crew made up of inexperienced, yet highly motivated individuals. By now I had replaced all the stolen equipment. It was a slow process to teach the Praise and Worship team how to stand up to praise God.

"You have young legs," I said encouragingly. "Why can't you stand up to praise God? I don't see any leg artery diseases or leg edema so you should be able to stand up for an hour. And even if you have a problem with your young legs - which you don't – I can always pray for healing so you can stand up to praise God without needing to sit down all the time."

A chorus of groans met me.

"But it has never been done before!" Credinescu said.

"But it will be done here!" I replied.

"It will never be accepted."

"It will be accepted when we start!"

"Furthermore, nobody knows these songs that we are singing," Credinescu mourned.

"They will be known," I said stubbornly. "I bought them from Australia."

"Who cares about Australia?" another boy said. "We are in Romania!"

"Let's just practice the songs and see how they come out."

"Are you sure we have to stand for practice too?" another voice perked up. "There's nobody here but us."

"This is to get you used to standing up," I said heartlessly. "If you, as a group, do not stand then how can I expect the congregation to stand? They will be looking to you for guidance. You will be modeling exemplary behavior for them!"

"We don't want to model behavior for them."

"You really don't have a choice. If you stand up at the front, people will look at you. And people model their behavior after what they see not what they hear."

"We will do what you say but we still don't believe that anybody will come to a church where they have to stand for so long and sing songs that they do not know!"

"Let's use our faith!" I reminded them. "Not just talk about it!"

....

A few weeks passed before another small obscure village church invited me to speak at one of its programs. I decided to bring my Praise and Worship team along. They had been practicing for some time now and were beginning to sound like a team. This would be a great chance for them to get their feet wet.

The church program was scheduled to start at 7:00 pm sharp. We arrived at 6:30 pm, and as we headed towards the church building, a man approached us.

"Are you the guest pastor that will be giving the message tonight?"

"Yes, and this is my Praise and Worship team."

He looked appalled. "We cannot let those girls who are wearing pants enter the church. You are welcome but they are not."

"What's wrong with their pants?" I asked.

"It is a sin to let women wear pants. We cannot let them desecrate the church sanctuary. I am surprised that you, as their pastor, would allow them to wear manly attire."

"They are dressed decently."

"They have to stay outside," the man said firmly. "And what's that you have there?"

"Those are our guitars, tambourines, and synthesizer."

"Surely you are not going to use those instruments from the devil in our church?" the man gasped.

"We use all types of instruments to praise God." I replied.

"You have to leave all the instruments outside. We cannot have those evil rock n' roll instruments polluting our holy place."

I turned towards my group.

"Do you sense that we are not welcome here? We don't need this. Let's go!"

"You told us that the senior pastor invited you here," Credinescu insisted. "We haven't even met him yet. Let's wait for him and see what he says before we go."

We didn't have to wait long, as the senior pastor soon came out to look for us.

"Why are you still out here?" he asked in astonishment. "Go inside! The program is about to begin and you still have to setup your equipment."

"We cannot go inside," I said, explaining our predicament. "This man says that some of us are not fit to enter the church."

"Never mind what he says. I invited you. Just go inside and I will talk to him."

We scurried into the church building under the disapproving gaze of the first man.

"Do any of you know who that man was?" I asked, as we hurriedly set up the equipment.

Everyone shook their heads.

"No idea. But let's praise and worship God anyway!"

As the Praise and Worship team praised and worshiped God, I noticed something which I had never seen before. People in the congregation were passing little slips of handwritten notes up front to the pulpit. It was like when I was back in grade school before the advent of mobile phones and instant text messages. Every time a paper reached the front, it would be intercepted by the pastor. He would open the paper, read it, and then put it into his pocket. The stream of papers hastened considerably when I stood up to preach. It was disconcerting. I wondered whether my fly was unzipped.

After I delivered my message, the senior pastor beckoned us to meet him outside. We complied dutifully.

"I suppose all of you would like to know why I have called you outside," he began.

We nodded unanimously.

"Well, it seems like that man whom you met earlier has organized a small revolt against all of you."

"A revolt?" I swallowed.

"Yes, he was encouraging other members of the church to complain and show their disapproval of your group's attire. Many of them did."

"Did they write their complaints on those little pieces of paper?"

"Yes, I read them all. Besides the clothing, they also complained that your group sang too loud, the songs were unknown and your group stood up too much."

"Don't blame my group," I responded. "They learned it all from me."

"It is not accepted here, especially the loud music!"

"OK, but I distinctly heard some members of your congregation yelling loudly when we were praying. Their yelling was much louder than any of the songs we sang!"

"Yes, they did. But that's different. The belief here is that yelling loudly makes one holy! Singing loudly does not. Also, only one of your group members brought a head covering but it was too small." His face turned a beetroot red. "Wearing pants, if you are female, is an insult to God Himself. Someone also complained that one of you is wearing makeup and jewelry. Furthermore, you moved your hands and feet too much while praising God. Nobody is allowed to move their bodies, feet, or hands while worshipping God!"

"I preached in many African and American churches before and their choirs move a lot. Many of them actually dance. Does that mean that they are all sinning?"

"Yes!"

"Did they condemn the message I gave, too?" I asked.

"The message was fine. But I did receive one note where a person expressed concern about the length of your hair. It appears that your hair is touching your ears and that is a sin too."

"Only one comment?" I said. "I must be doing fine then."

"Well, there were several comments that you smiled too much while delivering your message."

"My smiling offended them too?"

"Well, it is inappropriate. In the Bible, it was never mentioned that Jesus smiled. So we should not smile or make jokes at all."

I was about to retort that in the Bible, Jesus was never mentioned going to the bathroom either and that corollary, maybe we should not go to the bathroom either and be one happy, constipated family.

Instead I replied, "Well, thank you for inviting us here. We will now pack up our equipment and leave."

"I'm sorry for this to happen," the senior pastor replied. "I thought you knew what church is all about."

As we piled into the car, I turned around to address my thoroughly discouraged group.

"Sorry for all of this. Let us remember that what matters is what God thinks about us! We did everything for Him and with all our heart. We should focus on that."

I turned the ignition. It made a turning noise, but did not start. After several more cranks the engine still refused to turn over. I glanced out of the window and almost jumped out of my seat. The man that had originally criticized us was standing beside the car peering through the window.

"Yes?" I asked, rolling down the window.

"You can see that God is punishing you for your sssssins," the man hissed. "That is why your car won't start."

Needless to say, we never went back to that church.

ॐ∼ও

47. Start of Church

It was three days till opening day. I distributed 20,000 flyers in neighborhood letter boxes announcing the start of a brand new church. Learning from the crusades earlier, I avoided distributing in public places, out of concern that the school director would be similarly pressured and hence; resort to renege on his word, too.

All this while, the Praise and Worship team were meeting about twice a week for rehearsals.

"Are you excited about this weekend?" I asked. "Ready to stand up and praise God?"

"Yes, we are!" they chorused unanimously. "We can stand for ten hours with ease!"

"Do you remember when you told me that your legs would collapse if you stood for more than one hour?"

They laughed at that absurdity. "We are younger than you and can stand far longer than you."

"What a privilege to be given this chance to begin a new work here," I said. "Let's do a quick practice today."

The group hurriedly set up the equipment. Then something unexpected occurred.

"The microphones are not here!" Credinescu said, perplexed, looking through the bags. "Did you forget them at home?"

"I didn't touch the equipment since all of you met for prayer and praise last week," I said. "Search the bags again. They must be inside there somewhere."

We looked through the bags again but in vain.

"Did anybody see the microphones?" I asked.

"They were here last week during prayer," another young man replied.

"We all saw them then," Credinescu chimed in.

"Yes, we used the microphones," another voice confirmed. "They were all there."

"I wasn't at that meeting," I said. "Tell me what happened."

"Everything went really well," Credinescu said. "We practiced and then prayed before packing up the equipment. All of us were involved."

"But the microphones are not here now!" I pointed out.

It took a moment for the group to realize the significance of that.

Then it dawned on Credinescu. "Since the microphones are nowhere to be found and we packed the bags ourselves, which means one of us stole the microphones after the prayer finished last week!"

"That's incredible!" I exclaimed. "I cannot believe one of you will steal the microphones! And after prayer! And we start church in three days! Now we have no microphones, including the wireless one!"

"I didn't take it," Credinescu said.

"We didn't take it," the group echoed.

"Which one of you did it?" somebody asked.

They looked at one another helplessly which quickly turned hostile. Voices rang out.

"You took a great deal of interest in those microphones!" a voice accused.

"You were wearing pants with large pockets, large enough to hide microphones!"

"You had a jacket on with multiple pockets."

"I was praying not stealing!"

"You needed money so you stole the microphones!"

I had to stop the accusations and fast! It was tearing the group apart. I didn't know what to think. It was beyond my comprehension that somebody would steal the microphones after prayer.

"I'll take the blame," I said. "Stop accusing each other. We have no proof of who did it. We will start the church with no microphones. At least we still have the other equipment."

Till this day, we did not find out who stole all the microphones after prayer.

. . . .

Our first service attracted a total of about 100 visitors which quickly dwindled down to a handful.

"They do not like us," Credinescu said. "Our worship songs are strange. Furthermore, nobody would come to church in a dilapidated school gym while there are so many beautiful church buildings in this city! "

"Don't take this personally," I said. "We are breaking so many sacred traditions that it is impossible for us to be accepted immediately. We will just have to build this church one person at a time."

"That would take forever. We want to see fast church growth!"

"Yes, I want that too. But God is more interested in seeing us, as a group, grow up first."

"We understand that but we still want to see thousands come to Christ now!"

"I will pray for you to have more patience!" I said.

"Yes, I need patience," Credinescu replied. "And I need it now!"

. . . .

A few months after the church's official opening, we had the Christmas Eve program where everything came to a head. After breaking and entering, we discovered that we had no heat. Then the electricity went out. And the mother of all mistakes was when I discovered I had bought funeral candles for our Christmas program.

I held the yellow candles in my hand and looked at Credinescu.

"I don't care if these candles are for the dead. We are going to use them as they are all we have."

"But the people? And it is Christmas!" Credinescu exclaimed.

"Never mind! We are doing this for God, not for the people. Let's light up the candles anyway. It's so dark here that the people may not notice the color of the candles. Furthermore, the little flames may warm up this mausoleum-gym and bring a little cheer to it."

"Let's do it then."

We lit the candles, passed them out, and began to sing. Albeit there was only one acoustic guitar for accompaniment coupled with frozen fingers, we passed with flying colors.

The crowd shook their heads sadly at the candles and mumbled glacially, with frozen lips, at the unfamiliar Christmas carols. I gave a short message on the Messiah, the greatest gift ever given to mankind. The frostbitten crowd thought otherwise - they were thinking heat was the greatest gift to mankind. Then I made an unexpected announcement.

"I have some Christmas shoeboxes with me."

I explained the age requirements before handing out the brightly colored packages. The gym fell into a deep hush as the kids and youth received the love packets. For a moment, the biting cold was forgotten as kindness rekindled frigid eyes and hearts.

A young teenager approached me with her package.

"Can I really keep it?" she asked, her eyes wide open in disbelief and wonderment.

"Yes, it's yours," I said. "It is just some soap, toothbrush, something like that and probably a small toy."

"It doesn't matter what's inside. It's my *first present* ever. I am just so excited."

"You have never received a present in your whole life?"

She smiled sweetly. "No, this is my very first. Please say thank-you to the people who sent it."

I found that a little shoebox could open up a different world when put into the right hands.

Later that night, I found the guard who was supposed to open the gym for us. He was in a drunken stupor flat out in the basement of the grade school. By the flickering light of the candle, I noticed several empty bottles of alcohol by his side. But most of all, the small light lit up the huge smile on his face! I guess it was a good Christmas for him.

⊱⊰

48. Adventures in Church

Our church programs were often interrupted by unexpected events. Once when we were singing Michael W. Smith's, 'Let It Rain', a huge stone shattered the already broken windows of the school gym.

CRASH!

"Look out!" I shouted, as the rain of glass hurtled down on the congregation.

"AAAH!" somebody screamed.

Quick as a flash, I held up my Bible as a shield. In the back of my mind, I was wondering whether anyone in Romania had ever died while attending services at church. I could imagine the shocking headlines in tomorrow's newspapers – WOMAN GETS IMPALED THROUGH HEAD ATTENDING CHURCH! That would surely kill any little bit of enthusiasm that we had garnered for our little, startup church.

Fortunately, the shards of glass did not kill anybody. However, some girls did jump up and scream, shaking glass from their hair.

"Quick!" I shouted. "Outside! We'll catch the culprits who threw the stone!"

Credinescu was the first to react. He shook pieces of glass from his hair, like a dog after a shower, and ran for the gym's exit door. We collided at the door.

"What are you waiting for?' I exclaimed. "Get the door open."

Credinescu's voice sounded mournful, as he struggled with the door. "I cannot. It seems to be stuck!"

"You got to be joking with me!" I said. "Move aside and let me try!"

I grabbed the door knob and gave a mighty push expecting the door to yield. But the door held. We were losing precious time. At this rate, our rock-thrower would be miles away. I peered through the keyhole.

"I can see all types of wooden benches and tables piled up behind the door. It looks like somebody barred us in before stoning us!"

"Whoever he is, he's not stupid," Credinescu muttered. "He's giving himself time to escape. Let me try the door again."

He rushed the door with his shoulders. With a deafening boom, the door came off its hinges and the barricade behind it fell with a thundering crash. He clambered over the fallen furniture like a crab and raced outside the gym. I marveled at the number of overturned benches and tables that had been stacked up against the door. Somebody must really hate us, I thought.

"Do you see anybody?" I asked, as I emerged out into the school courtyard.

"There's nobody here," Credinescu mouthed between clenched teeth. "If I catch the person who did this, I will …"

We searched the courtyard together. It was futile, the person was long gone.

"I'm going to search outside the school grounds," I said.

"I'll come with you," Credinescu said.

We walked out of the school gates to where we had parked our cars. There was no sign of anybody. But something else caught my eye.

"Somebody smashed my windshield!' I exclaimed.

Credinescu stood in silent rage as we stared at the large hole directly in the center of my windshield. Broken glass was everywhere.

"I cannot believe that somebody would do this to you!" Credinescu choked.

I was still too stunned to respond. I unlocked the car and looked around for the stone that must have entered the car but found none.

"There's no stone in the car!" I said wearily.

Credinescu stared at me.

"That means that the windshield was smashed in with something other than a stone," he surmised. "Something like a long iron pipe. Somebody really hates you. But I have more bad news for you."

"What?"

"It seems like that person may have slashed your tires, too! One of your tires is completely flat."

I walked around the car inspecting it. "I would be surprised if they only slashed one! The people really hate us doing church here, don't they?"

"Not us, only you," Credinescu said. "My car is fine. Are you going to call the police?"

"I don't see anyone here," I replied. "What are the police going to do? Anyway, I only have basic coverage on my car. It only covers third party damages. The police report is not going to help either. I don't think that any more damage will be done to this car today. Let's go back inside and finish up the church program."

Credinescu took a last look at my vehicle.

"I'm glad that is not my car!"

I sighed deeply.

ॐ∼ॐ

49. Our Church

Daliascu was the Romanian karate champion three years in a row. When I first met her she was beating up a few boys in the street.

I interrupted her fight. "I'm starting a church here in the neighborhood. I would like to invite you to come."

"What are you doing in my neighborhood?" Daliascu challenged. The boys that she had beaten up scrammed as fast as their puny legs could carry them. They were very glad of this unforeseen intervention.

"I live here too, so this is also my neighborhood," I replied, calmly.

She showed me her fist. "You are on my turf and I can beat you up or down anytime."

"I am not afraid of you. And I don't want your turf. I am inviting you to church."

"Why would I want to go to church? They are hypocrites! All of them!"

"This church will be different!" I persisted. "Come, and you will see."

"I went with a friend to church once and they threw me out because I had pants on. Do you know who I am? I represent Romania at international competitions! I win gold medals for this country and they chase me out of church! I have never felt so humiliated in my whole life. I will never go back to church."

"We don't care whether you have pants or a skirt on. But it would be nice if you came with one or the other! We are not a nudist church."

She laughed and dropped her fierce attitude and challenge.

"I might just come then. But don't expect me to like it!"

"You don't have to like it."

"I'm sure I won't."

....

Panseluta was another girl I met in the neighborhood. Medium length hair, smart, and full of filial piety - she was every mother's dream of a perfect daughter. I approached her one afternoon.

"Would you like to come to church?" I asked.

"What type of church?" she asked, suspiciously.

"A non-denominational church."

"What's that? All churches belong to a denomination! Are you from some weird cult?"

"No, it's not a cult!" I exclaimed. "The church I started is more modern, that's all."

"I don't believe you! You are trying to make me join a cult. Do I have to drink blood or something?"

"No! Just come and you will see. You may actually like it."

Panseluta shuddered at the thought. "My uncle is a priest. I have no need to go to church."

"That's not the same!" I exclaimed. "A priest is not God."

"Are you a priest?' she inquired.

"No, I'm a pastor and I'm inviting you to church."

"I'm not going to your church and that's final. My uncle told me many times before that if I were to leave my denomination I will go to hell. Why would I want to go to hell?"

"I don't want you to go to hell. And I don't want you to change your denomination either."

"Then why would I want to come to your church?"

I scratched my head for any answer. "Because it may be fun and you might learn something new."

"I like to learn," she conceded.

"So you will come?"

"No! I am not coming to your church!" she said, and stormed off.

A few days later, I met Panseluta again.

"Would you like to come to church?" I asked pleasantly.

"No, I don't want to go to your church," she replied.

"Why don't you bring a friend then?"

"If I don't want to go to your church, why would I bring a friend? If you ask me again, I will scream! Can't you get that into your head? I will never come to your church."

"Are you sure?" I asked.

"You are so persistent - like a mosquito."

"You can swat me if you come to church."

"I might do just that."

. . . .

Zambilescu was about nineteen, wore glasses, had shoulder length hair and a cute angelic face. I met her at the local corner coffee shop.

"I started a church," I began. "It's a place where you can worship God."

"I like to go to church," Zambilescu said. "What denomination are you?"

"We are non-denominational and we welcome everybody," I replied. "We are friendly, open, and we sing great songs."

"My father would never allow me to go to such a welcoming, friendly church."

"What do you mean?"

"The church I go to is very strict and controlling. My father would kill me if I come to your church."

"You can ask him to come with you."

Zambilescu nearly fainted at that idea. "He would rather die than leave his church! What would his friends think of him? They would call him a traitor. That is unthinkable!"

"Maybe he would allow you to come by yourself, then."

"Never!" Zambilescu gasped. "What would his friends in church think of him if he goes to church without his entire family? Tongues would start wagging. He would be questioned by the elders."

"Maybe you shouldn't come to church, then."

"What do you mean?"

"If your father is so strict, then it's better that you do not come. I don't want you to get into trouble with him."

"I can tell my father that I went for a walk," Zambilescu said slyly, her eyes opening wide behind her glasses.

"So?" I didn't follow.

"I can tell my father I went for a long walk. That walk may take me to your church. That way I can avoid telling my father the truth, but at the same time not lie to him."

It was my turn to gasp.

....

The hair on Trandafirescu's head resembled a field of wheat that had been blown backwards by a fiery dust storm. Every strand stood on end and was bent backwards in a petrified manner. Unfortunately, her face mirrored her hair in a petrified dread-look that was most unsuitable for her. It was her first visit to my church.

"Can you please pray for me?" she begged. "The doctors have sent me home to die."

"What's the matter with you?" I asked.

"I went for a medical check-up and they discovered that I have stomach and liver cancer. The doctors say that there is no hope for me.'

"Do you attend church anywhere?"

"Sometimes I go to a church near where I live," Trandafirescu replied.

"Did they pray for you?" I asked.

"I asked, but the pastor told me that God had given me this disease to humble me. You see, I have not been the best wife or the best mother. My children are into drugs and have left home. My husband is a drunk because of me. My pastor told me that God had allowed this to come on me as a lesson. What shall I do? I don't want to die. I want to raise my children and be a good wife. Please tell me whether you will pray for me."

I opened my eyes wide.

"God didn't give you this cancer," I said. "That's for sure. No Father would do that to His child. Do you believe that God can heal you?"

"I want to believe but maybe I deserve this as punishment."

"God doesn't have to punish you to heal you."

She cried abundantly as we prayed for her healing. Then wiping the tears from her petrified face, she whispered, "I have scheduled a complete checkup with some specialists in another city tomorrow."

"Call me and tell me the results," I said.

Sure enough, the next day I received a phone call from Trandafirescu.

"They examined me thoroughly and found nothing!" she whooped. "No cancer! Nothing! They were very puzzled with the results from the other examination. They told me that it was impossible for me to be healed. But I know better!"

"Praise God!" I said. "To Him, there's no difference between healing cancer or a headache. One is not bigger or harder than the other. Jesus is the Great Physician and nothing is impossible for Him."

"I want to come to your church," she shouted into the phone.

"You know where we are," I replied.

The next time I saw her, her face had already begun to thaw. Her hair, however, was the same.

．．．．．．．．．．．．．．．．．．．．．．．．．

Brinzescu could have been Charlie Chaplin's twin except for the missing moustache. The same pants, oversized shoes, jacket and hat – it was all there.

"Is this a church?" he drawled. "And can I stay for awhile?"

"Yes, this is a church and we are very glad you are here," I said.

"Listen!" Brinzescu said, and then belched loudly. The liquor on his breath could have overwhelmed an adult wildebeest.

I took five steps backwards voluntarily.

"Listen," he said again, his face flushed with alcohol. "I have no family. You don't mind if I stay and listen to the songs and the message today, do you?"

"Not at all," I replied. "You are always welcome. What happened to your family?"

"They all left me. They called me a drunk and then left me. My wife was the last to leave, but she left me, too, for another man. I am all alone now."

"We can be your family."

He put his hand on my shoulder and tried to drag me closer. I resisted, fighting back.

"I have no family, but if you can let me stay, I will appreciate it very much. I walked a long way and almost had a seizure on the road here."

"Do you have any other church closer to where you are living?" I asked. "That way you will not need to walk so far."

He burst into a fit of inebriated laughter. "Plenty of churches where I live! Churches on every street corner."

I waited.

"Plenty of churches but find me one that will let me enter!"

"Why won't they let you enter?" I asked stupidly.

"Because I'm a drunk! And they don't like drunks!"

"But I thought that the church should help people."

"There are thousands like me and nobody helps us! We are all alone. Nobody cares about us."

"Come here anytime. We welcome you and everyone like you."

. . . .

Musculouscu was short, but broader than the love seat he was occupying. His T-shirt groaned and shrieked from the enormous muscles it had to cover. I expected it to tear at any moment, but miraculously it held on.

In the quiet room, Musculouscu inspected me the way a mountain would inspect the goat walking on it.

"Where are you from?" he finally asked, flexing his biceps.

"From America," I said, weakly.

"I have been there once," he replied. "And to Asia twice."

I raised my eyebrows, wondering where he was going with this.

"Competition! I was in those places for the world bodybuilding championships."

"Ah!" I nodded.

"I am the five-time Romanian bodybuilding champion!" He flexed his biceps again.

"Aah!" I nodded more vigorously.

"What are you doing in my girlfriend's house?" he asked.

"I came to see her parents," I replied quickly. "Her father is sick and wants prayer. That's why I'm here."

He turned to his girlfriend who was occupying a small part of the love seat. She had been quiet as a mouse

"Is that true?"

His girlfriend nodded.

He calmed down. "Would you like to see some of my pictures?"

I didn't want to but I said, "I would love to."

Without a word, his girlfriend got up, and fetched the pictures. Musculouscu insisted that I see all his championship poses. As it turned out, it was very impressive especially since he was only inches away.

"How did you get those stomach muscles?" I asked. "I used to work out, too, but could never get those ten-pack abs. I never managed more than four."

Musculouscu smiled widely. "Since you helped my girlfriend's father, I am going to help you. I will train you so you can get those abdominal muscles."

"You want to be my personal trainer?" I gasped.

"Yes, I told you that I will help you because you helped my girlfriend's father."

"Do I have to do ten thousand sit-ups and crunches every day?"

"No, only thirty but in a few sets."

"Only thirty to get those abs?" I asked incredulously.

"There's a secret," he replied. "But I'll teach you."

"Funny thing about muscles though," I said. "They get covered with fat as one gets older. Everybody admires us now, but who will care about us when our muscles turn flaccid. Who will care about us then? Who will care about you?"

Musculouscu froze. He had never thought about that before.

"What do you mean by that?"

"Let me share with you about Jesus. He will always care about us even when we are fat and old."

After thirty minutes of sharing, Musculouscu wanted prayer.

"You will pray with us," he said to his girlfriend.

She nodded hurriedly and we prayed together.

"Now let me tell you about church," I said. "It's something different and you may like it."

....

Afaceriscu was a businessman. Intelligent to a fault, decisive and to the point, he wanted a formula for success. I had met him at a local businessmen's meeting.

"If I tithe, God will bless it, and I will receive many times over. Isn't that right?"

"You have it right and wrong," I replied.

He didn't like that. "Come to the point. Is that right or wrong?"

"Tithing is not a formula for success," I explained. "Tithing is a way whereby you put God first in your life. It is not so much about your money, but about your heart. It's almost like a test of your heart, about what's really important to you."

"But if I tithe, I will receive back, right? For example, if I have ten cars, then I can tithe a car, and God will multiply that, right?"

"Your way of thinking is not correct. As I said before, it is more of a test of whether you can put God first in your life. If you have ten cars and you tithe one - that is great. However, if you only have one car, with only the promise of additional cars, then you can still tithe that one car. It's much easier to tithe one when you have ten, than to tithe the first one and to believe God for the rest. You put God first and He blesses you back. The Israelites learned that at Jericho."

"I never thought about it that way before. I would like to place God first but I still want my tithe to multiply."

"Come to church and I will teach you more," I said. "You will learn that not only will the tithe multiply, but the remainder multiplies too, as it has now been redeemed."

"I will come to your church," Afaceriscu said. "That sounds interesting."

"But there's no formula," I warned him.

༈་༈

50. Petuniascu the Powerful

"That was the best message I have ever heard in my life," Petuniascu remarked.

"Praise God!" I replied.

"I have been to many churches and have heard many messages. That was the best. God touched my heart!"

I stood still, bewildered, and stared at the woman who was paying me all these compliments.

Petuniascu was the wife of a local minister and I had met her through her husband at a church function. Standing approximately 5'3" with a round tummy and a round face – the face accentuated by round glasses and round shoulder length hair, she looked at me with puppy dog eyes in admiration.

"Thank God I found your church," she continued on. "You showed God's grace to us. We are so thankful that you started a church here. We want to be here in your church forever. We want our children and our children's children to grow up here at your church. You are such a blessing from God to us."

I didn't know what to say. I had only done my duty.

"You are doing such a magnificent job here. But I have something to ask you."

"Yes?"

Petuniascu's fawn-like adoration turned coy.

"I have noticed for some time now that you like to mix with sinners. Now they are attending this church. Drunks, weightlifters, karate people, businessmen! They have no right to be here. Why do you want to mix with sinners? They are so dirty and not at all like us. A man of your standing and caliber must be very careful - only to be seen in good company. These sinners are no good. They drink, curse, smoke, lie, steal, dress like whores, and sleep around. You don't want them to infect you with their sin. You should keep yourself pure and avoid these people. That way God can use you mightily here in Romania."

I looked at her in amazement. She sounded so genuine in her remarks that I wondered if I needed to have my ear wax removed. Possibly I had heard wrong. I didn't know I had standing nor caliber, and I didn't know that mixing with sinners could infect me with sin.

"I beg your pardon?" I said. "Can you please repeat that?"

She smiled. "You heard right: If you mix with sinners, God will punish you and your ministry will die. But if you avoid all these dirty people, God will bless you. I know this country and you do not. Listen to me."

"Didn't Jesus mix with sinners?"

"I know that," Petuniascu said in an exasperated voice. "But you are not Jesus."

"I know I am not Jesus," I replied.

She nodded. "Good! Let me explain it to you. Imagine that you are a man walking down a street. As you are walking, you suddenly spot another man who had fallen into a ditch. You stop, reach out your arm to help pull this man out, but instead, the fallen man in the ditch pulls you in with him. Don't you see? It is so much easier for the fallen man to pull you into the ditch then for you to pull him out. So if you mix with sinners, you will be pulled into their folds."

"I appreciate your care and know what you are telling me but God called me here to get sinners saved. I didn't come here to start a church for Christians."

"But you cannot be serious. Look at them and look at us. They are so bad and ugly. God hates these people and you should too."

"God doesn't hate these people, only their sin."

Petuniascu played her trump card. "I have many friends and we will all come to your church. I like your preaching and I will tell all my friends. We will fill up your church. But you must not let sinners in otherwise we will not come."

It was a sweet temptation. "I'm sorry but I intend to follow the vision God gave to me for this nation. I will continue to mix with sinners and show them the love of Jesus."

Petuniascu got angry. "If you do not listen to what I say, you will lose power. God will take away your power because you choose to be with sinners. Come to think of it, maybe that is why your message this time was not so strong as some of your previous messages. You are becoming infected!"

"Thank God that I am losing power," I replied. "Because when I have no power of my own, God will be able to show His power."

"Your church will fail for sure!" Petuniascu cursed. "None of my friends will come to your church."

"It may fail, but I guarantee you that some sinners will be set free first."

"You are really stupid to believe that you can change them."

"I'm not doing anything," I replied. "It's the Holy Spirit that will do the changing."

"You are young and naïve," Petuniascu smiled again. "As a foreigner, you may think you know this country but you do not know it at all. I will help you become the biggest pastor in this country if you will let me guide you. I can help you tremendously."

"I may be young, naïve and become the smallest pastor in this country. But as long as I do what God has called me to do, then I have accomplished my mission."

Petuniascu tossed her round head. "Since you are too stupid to see and avoid sinners, I will have to find another church to go to. Of course, I will have to take my friends with me."

"Would you like me to drive you there?" I asked.

Petuniascu scowled. "I will do everything in my power to see that you fail! I will even call your pastor back in America and tell them about your rebellious insistence to meet with sinners. They will agree with me."

I gulped some more.

කැ·ණ

51. Conversations with God III

I took this up with my Father as soon as I could.

"Am I doing something wrong?" I asked. "Could Petuniascu be correct? After all, I am a foreigner in this country."

"You have to break your fear of rejection by other people. The fear of other people's opinions many times governs your actions. I know you want to be liked by other people, but if you listen to them you may forget what I have told you. King Saul chose to listen to the voices of his army captains and bring back alive the enemy king as well as the finest animals. The enemy king, Agag, produced an heir that culminated many, many years later in Haman, the Agag-ite, who almost managed to single-handedly wipe out the entire Jewish race if not for the intervention by Queen Esther. One act of disobedience by King Saul had dire consequences for the whole nation of Jews hundreds of years later. Similarly, Moses did not enter into the Promised Land himself because he listened to the voice of the people.

"What may sound perfectly logical and good to you may bring great destruction later on. For the voice of man may be logical, but My voice is truth. Man may be fair but I am just. Men's laws can never supersede My laws. Following the voice of man instead of My voice is counted as disobedience, no matter how good the intentions are. For to obey is better than sacrifice, and to heed is better than the fat of rams."

"I understand that but Petuniascu is the wife of a local leader," I reasoned. "She has wide influence. I have none. Surely growing a church her way cannot be bad."

"Do not look at the outside. Saul became king because the people looked at his stature. He was strong and was a head taller than any other person. Yet I rejected Saul as king to the disappointment of all. For I do not look at the things man looks at. Man looks at the outward appearance, but I look at the heart.

"Learn that hypocrites are the worst type of human beings. They use my Word as an end to control and manipulate; to condemn, judge, and kill. Worst of all, they use it to preach a different gospel than the one I showed. To preach a different gospel is not half good. It cannot be defended on grounds that at least some truth is being preached. Because to preach a different gospel is to preach no gospel at all.

"If you listen to hypocrites, you will discover an alternate road to redemption. While not denying Christ, ecclesiastical rules supported by My Word are added. This in turn leads to self-righteousness and pride manifested by external appearances and conduct. They are whitewashed tombs, all beautiful on the outside, but full of putrefaction on the inside. Of paramount importance to them is the face presented to the public – unblemished, covered, dissembling humility, sanctimonious insincerity, and false holiness. Unfortunately, the private, inward transformation is missing. Subtly but surely, the rules and the law become more important than My grace. They shut the kingdom of heaven in men's faces. They themselves do not enter, nor will they let those enter who are trying to. For salvation is only by Jesus' blood. It was poured out for all sinners. None can earn salvation for none deserve it. It is a free gift and it paid for your debt in full.

"Look at the man in the back of your church, blinking back tears, who just gave his life to Me after a lifetime of rebellion; look at that woman, happy tears washing away her mascara, coming to the saving knowledge that I love her more than any other man ever could. And inside each of them, I find another home. Look at that instead."

52. Surviving Christianity

I tried to look at that, but it was hard. After a few months of sharing the unconditional love of Christ, a familiar theme emerged.

"What happened to your face?" I asked Zambilescu, one Sunday morning.

She turned her face away and would not answer me.

"You can tell me," I urged. "We are your friends here."

Tears welled up in her eyes. "My father punched me in the face for coming to your church. I hate him! I hate him!"

I took a deep breath. This had always been my worst nightmare.

"I went back home after church last week and he caught me as I entered. He asked me where I had been. I didn't want to lie so I told him that I have been to your church. He shouted at me and commanded me never to go to your cult-church ever again. I challenged him and he punched me. I have never been so scared in my life."

"What happened then? Did he calm down?"

"He ordered me to tell you that I am not allowed to come to church anymore. If I do not get back home in half an hour, he said he would kill me. I am so afraid. What shall I do?"

"For now, listen to your father," I replied.

"But he punched me in the face! Why should I listen to him? I want to run away."

"Because he is still your father. That is why you should listen to him. When you are older, then you can make decisions regarding whether to stay or leave. For now, just go back home."

"But that means I can never come back here again," Zambilescu cried.

"Don't worry," I said, full of worry. "We will always be your family even if you are not here."

....

Another Sunday, another story, but with the same theme. It was Trandafirescu's turn. Her face was even more petrified than her hair as she dragged me into a corner.

"I need to talk to you," she said urgently.

"Yes?" I inquired.

"My husband found out that I'm going to church."

"So?"

"He says if I go to church he will leave me! What shall I do?"

"But you told me you had visited a different church before. Why is he leaving you now?"

"He says that your church is from the devil. He says that if I want to waste my time, then I might as well go back to the other church. He doesn't like the other church, either, but he really hates your church. Somebody told him that we raise our hands and clap in worship here. He says that you only do that at football games, not in church. What shall I do?"

This was a difficult one.

"Why don't I come to your house and talk to your husband?" I said finally.

"Oh, no! He would rather die than meet with you! He really hates you."

"But he doesn't even know me," I pointed out. "I have never met your husband in my entire life."

"That doesn't matter. I got healed and he cannot stand that. Now I can go back to work and make some money. I know now it was not my fault I had cancer. He doesn't like that at all because now I am not under his feet. But I still don't want him to leave me!"

"I understand. You have to make up your mind on this matter. Pray for him."

"Pray for that drunk?"

"Yes, God can soften his heart towards you. Or change your reaction towards him."

"I'll try but I don't know about the results!"

"Just try and you will see."

....

As the months progressed, I prayed for sufficient grace to cover the abuses my congregation received for receiving Jesus Christ as their Lord and Savior.

Daliascu had never cried before, but she could not help blinking back tears. One of her eyes was puffy.

"Did your dad beat you?" I asked.

"He came home drunk one night and used me as a punching bag."

I swallowed hard. This trend was getting worse.

"He cursed me for going to church then cursed God. He beat me and threw me again and again against the concrete wall. He knocked my head back until I bounced off the wall. Then he punched me in the eye several times. He boxed my ears and I could not hear for weeks. I still cannot hear properly."

"Does he do this only when he's drunk?"

"No! Even when he's not drunk! He says that becoming a Christian is the worst thing I could ever do in my life! Now I am an outcast of the family. If he beats me again…."

"Yes?"

"I am the Romanian champion in karate. If he punches me again, I am going to kill him. I can kill him with just one move! Do you want me to demonstrate?"

"That's OK," I replied hurriedly. "Let me tell you what to do.'

"What do I do?" Daliascu asked.

"When your dad beats you, you take it."

"What? Are you crazy?"

"Yes, you heard right. You take it! Not because you are weak or you cannot take him out with a single blow to the neck. But you take it because you are now a Christian!"

It was then that Daliascu genuinely cried for the first time in her life.

....

Panseluta strode up to me and I turned to smile at her. But she was not smiling.

"My father threw me out of his home," she said quietly. "Where am I to go? I have no place to stay."

"Why did he throw you out?" I asked, knowing the answer well beforehand.

"Because I defied him and continued coming to your church. My uncle, who's a priest, told him that I was now destined for hell. Anyone who leaves the denomination automatically goes straight to hell. So my dad kicked me out and threw my Bible in the dumpster. He said I had no right to read the Bible."

"Are you sure there's no chance to talk to your dad - to make him see some sense?"

"There is no talking to him!"

"Well, if that's the case, maybe you can sleep for a few nights with somebody from the church. Then we can decide what to do. Your dad may calm down by then."

"He's coming after you next," Panseluta said. "He is huge and very, very angry!"

My eyes turned bigger than two pancakes.

....

Brinzescu, the drunk, sidled up to me in church. His breath would have shattered an alcohol breathalyzer into smithereens.

"I cannot come to church anymore!" he breathed on me.

"Are you sure?" I asked, getting intoxicated from the fumes.

"Yes! I have lost my house and I have to move away. I've come to church for months now and I've had prayers. You pray for salvation at the end of every church meeting and I pray along with you. You pray for deliverance for me, but I cannot seem to stop drinking. When my landlord found out that I was a Christian, he threw me out. I'm going to go away for awhile for treatment."

"Are you moving far away?"

"Yes, very far away."

"If you ever come back to this city, make sure you stop by. You will always be a part of us."

Brinzescu cried, the tears dripping down the exposed veins on his cheeks to his oversized smelly clothes. "Nobody has ever accepted me before except for this church. And now I have to go away!"

....

Afaceriscu, his shoulders slumped in defeat, gripped my hand tightly.

"God is still in control, right?"

"He is in control," I assured him. "Last time I checked, He was still on the throne."

"I had to close down my business. My debtors closed in. I wanted to start tithing but now I cannot. Do you think God will forgive me? I really wanted to give Him the first of my firstfruits, but now I have nothing to give at all."

"God never needed your money. What He wants is your heart. You may have lost all but you gained your soul back."

"I never thought I would win losing."

. . . .

As for Musculouscu, the body building champ, he had no trouble at all. Every time I close my eyes, I can clearly see the ripples of his biceps in my mind. I guess when you have biceps twice the size of other people's thighs; you would not have trouble either.

53. What's Wrong With You, Woman?

The young boy had a red, sad-horse face. His shirt was buttoned right up to his throat, slowly strangling him. Maybe that accounted for the redness of his face. I wasn't sure.

"May I help you?" I asked pleasantly.

"I have to talk to you," he said, cornering me. He sounded furious. His tight collar was not helping.

"That's what I'm here for."

He snapped his teeth at me angrily. "Why did you allow that woman to share today? Women are not allowed to speak or teach in the church. It is forbidden by Saint Paul. You are sinning against God and profaning the sacred grounds of the church by this sacrilegious act of liberalism. You should repent before the whole church for your actions today. We believed in you as a pastor and you have let us down!"

I was horrified to hear that I was sinning again. I have never sinned so much in my life until after the church began. I must be the king of sinners in Romania according to all the reports I have been hearing.

"I didn't know that women cannot share in the church! Furthermore, that woman was sharing her testimony on how God brought her through her difficulties. I am sure it was very encouraging for others!"

"Paul preached against it. Women are to remain silent at all times! It's in the book of Corinthians and again in Timothy. Are you going against the Bible's teaching?"

"You have to understand the cultural and supracultural aspects of the Bible to understand completely what Paul was trying to say. In that time, people congregated in a physical space and questioned the preachers by shouting out questions. It was not becoming for women to shout out loud, especially in public. Also, Paul was contrasting the authority of men and the usurping of it by women."

He stamped his foot angrily and cut me off. "There are no cultural elements in the Bible. You are just giving excuses for your mistake."

"So if women are not allowed to teach or share, then what do you think women are for?"

"Well...well, women should stay at home," he stammered. "That's their place. They must not sin and earn and stay in their salvation by having many children."

"Earn their salvation by having children? Where did you learn that from? I know you didn't learn it from me."

"It's in the Bible too. I can show you that in Timothy. Don't you ever read the Bible?"

"I know where it is," I sighed. "Childbearing there means that it is through women that Jesus will come into this world. As to your earlier comment on this place being holy, let me remind you that this is a public school. There is nothing sacred about this place! If you come here tomorrow you will hear boys and girls cursing and beating up each other. We just rent this place weekends for church meetings."

"And another thing!" he steamrolled on, without hearing my explanations.

"Yes?"

"I noticed that the woman was also wearing gold earrings! How could you allow her to wear that? She will influence all the other girls in the church to wear jewelry! That does not please God when women adorn and beautify themselves. I want you to speak to that woman and rebuke her. She is a great sinner."

I didn't know what to say. He seemed so earnest. I thought for awhile before replying.

"Please explain something to me. If women cannot beautify themselves, does that include banning soap, deodorant, toothpaste, and shampoo for them? Or is it God's will that women be toothless, stinky, and have wild hair?"

"You should get on your knees and repent before God for your sins!" he harrumphed, choking on his collar. "I don't have to answer your questions. You are not following God's word! That is all that matters."

54. The Art of Pilfering

At about that time, a new neighborhood multi-purpose convenience store, the EURO, opened for business. Stepping through its doors, one was immediately struck by piles of goods stacked haphazardly together on makeshift shelves. In my mind, it should have avalanche warnings posted. On the positive side, one could buy almost anything there. It was not unusual to find sausages on top of toilet bowls or mothballs next to chocolate balls. The arrangement of items did not have to make sense. It was the only store in the neighborhood and had absolute monopoly power.

I was not too concerned about the store's layout. I was only too thankful that I could finally buy vegetables without having to grow them and buy meat without having to raise my own animals. All my education in America had not prepared me for a self-sustaining lifestyle. That was why I was not too concerned about the store's insane layout.

Today, I was shopping for some soft drinks.

"What would you like?" the store assistant asked, indicating a wall of liquids.

I stared at the wall. Everything from lemon juice to lemon scented toilet bowl cleaner was there.

"Give me a minute!" I said, my eyes sorting out the poisonous from the non-poisonous.

The assistant continued to stare at me, well versed in the art of catching shoplifters. I felt her eyes microscopically dissecting my every movement.

I was looking at some peach drink when a sudden commotion broke out at the entrance doors. All eyes in the store, including the assistant, turned towards this noise.

A group of about eight gaily dressed gypsies had entered the store. As I stared, one man who had a violin began playing a lively jig. The seven women with him immediately began twirling and dancing in rhythm to the sprightly music. For a minute, it seemed that the EURO store was taken over by a lively stage show.

"What's happening?" I asked in amazement.

"They are just begging," the shop assistant replied. "But with some music as incentive."

"They're pretty good!" I added.

"Music is in their blood," the assistant commented. "Dancing too!"

Shopping was forgotten as shoppers crowded around the gypsies watching their antics. I admired their rainbow-colored skirts, dresses and head shawls.

Then amid the vivacious strains of the violin all hell, literally, broke loose.

A woman screeched at the top of her voice. "THIEVES! HELP!" She shouted like somebody had stuck a knife in between her ribs.

"THIEVES!" she shouted, pointing down an aisle with a shaky finger.

We all looked to where she was pointing.

A fat, gypsy woman had slipped, unnoticed, into the store while all of us were watching the gay troupe of dancers and musician. As we focused on the troupe, she had been focused on stuffing items from the shelves down her ample bosom, aprons, and skirt.

She looked up in alarm. Before anybody could react, she rushed toward the exit doors. With one accord, the band seeing that their scheme had been exposed, ran pell-mell for the same doors. Galvanized by the fleeing gypsies, the store assistants ran for the same doors as well.

"Stop them!" a customer shouted, not lifting a finger to help.

The gypsies and the store assistants collided at the doors which flew open spewing the tide into the street. The fat gypsy woman, leaking sausages and chunks of cheese, bowled everybody over as she fled down the street. The rest of the band followed. The assistants did not have a chance.

"What happened?" I asked stupidly.

"Didn't you see it?" one shop assistant said angrily, picking herself up. "They just robbed us. They distracted us with all the song and dance while one of them cleaned out the shelves. The boss will be so mad when he finds out what happened. All our salaries will be reduced by the amount the gypsies stole."

"But it was not your fault," I pointed out.

"It does not matter," she said, shaking with a mixture of fear and fury. "We have to pay back for everything! At this rate, we will have no salary at all."

"Does this happen often?"

"Never at this store before! We know it happens at bars. The gypsies distract the drunks with hugs, music, kisses and then pick their pockets. But those are drunks and they are easy prey. I cannot believe they managed to fool us! It's just stealing by distraction. They may bump into you when you are at the ATM or on the bus. As one of them apologizes to you profusely and while your attention is diverted, the other one picks your pockets clean. Mostly, they are after cash and mobile phones. But sausages and cheese? "

"A modern version of the artful Dodger and Oliver," I muttered.

"What's that you said?" she asked.

"Nothing," I replied hurriedly.

"Thieving is hereditary with them!"

"Let's not generalize."

"Yes, they may be nice to you at first to allay your suspicions. Then when your guard is down, they will rob you blind! They cannot be trusted! Here comes the boss now."

"I will come back for the juice later," I said. "I think I see a ball of cheese on the street. Don't you think it wise to retrieve it?"

The shop assistant hurried off to recover the ball of cheese.

55. I Want To Eat Some Roof Too

"God help us!" Credinescu shouted. "You nearly sent that bride to heaven!"

With a screeching of rubber, I swung the car violently back onto the highway. The smell of burnt rubber assailed my nose, the taste of cold sweat assailed my mouth, and Credinescu's shouts assailed my ears. Any more sensory assailments and I would end up a basket case.

A horse had suddenly ran onto the highway! I pulled sharply to the left to avoid it. In doing so, I had nearly killed a bride, all dressed in white, walking on the other side of the highway. It took me a few moments to calm the hammering in my heart.

"I was just trying to avoid the horse," I breathed.

"It would be funny had you avoided the horse and killed the bride instead," Credinescu replied.

"She should have more horse sense!" I protested. "You cannot walk on the highway! The horse is, after all, a horse and wouldn't know any better. The bride is not a horse."

"Didn't you see the bride and her entourage?" Credinescu persisted.

"I saw them but my mind was slow. Seeing horses running on the highway affects me that way. Then the bride all dressed in white ... but isn't the highway just for vehicles?"

Credinescu eyed me like an alien. "You should know! You have been driving here long enough!"

"I would like to know what they are doing on the highway!" I pleaded.

"The horse or the bride?"

"Let's start with the bride."

"It's simple. She is getting married and she is walking to church."

"But why is she on the highway?"

"The village roads are really muddy and the bride does not want to get her wedding dress all dirty. The highway is sort-of paved so it's a logical choice."

"And the horse? Don't tell me it's part of the bridal train!"

"Oh no! That horse looks abandoned. Did you see its ribs and flanks sticking out? It probably was grazing by the road, got startled and accidentally ran onto the highway."

"No, I did not see its ribs, I was busy trying not to kill it. But why would anybody abandon a horse?"

"Gypsies do it when they are unable to feed their horses anymore or when it gets too old to pull their carts. They work the horses, sometimes starving them, often beating them senseless, and then, one day just abandoning them."

"That sounds awful. But why are you so sure they are gypsies?"

"That's what they do!" Credinescu replied matter-of-factly. "But I hear that there is a new law banning all horse drawn carts from the highways. This will be a nationwide ban. If the farmers, who are not gypsies, cannot use the highways, they will abandon their horses too. Often times, the only way for farmers to get to their farmland is by using the highway."

"But why don't they use country roads instead? Don't they know how dangerous it is on the highway?"

"They would but unfortunately, there are no country roads. You can't simply take your horse through somebody's front yard to get to your plot of farmland! I predict a multitude of abandoned horses very soon."

"That's not very helpful for drivers. The government should construct some country roads."

"The government is more concerned about the size of their paychecks than country roads. Jesus will be back before these rural roads are built!"

I thought it wise to change the subject. "So tell me about the church we are visiting today."

"Well, it is a gypsy church located near the mountains. The people there are very poor. There are several hundred gypsies in the camp itself. The church has about twenty people. They do not have a pastor and will appreciate a message from you."

"I hope it will not be like some of the other churches we visited before!"

"No! No! This will be quite different."

"This will be my first visit to a gypsy church," I said. "How did this church get started?"

"Some Americans started it after the fall of Communism but left some time back. There is a Romanian leader there who maintains the church. He does his best but it's not easy because the gypsies have their own culture and rules."

"Sounds challenging to me," I muttered.

....

We arrived at the gypsy camp, after driving through craters of mud, right into a cacophony of shouts and screams.

"Sounds like a mob," I said. "I hope they are not going to chase us away. We just arrived."

"This probably has nothing to do with us," Credinescu replied. "We are on the outskirts of the camp. The church is further inside. Let me find out what's happening."

He was back in a few minutes.

"There was a man chained to a makeshift chimney! They discovered him there this morning."

"There was a man chained to a chimney?"

"Yes, he had a fight with some other gypsies and they dragged him there and chained him to the chimney."

"How long was he chained there?"

"I don't know, but long enough for him to eat some chunks of the roof."

"You cannot be serious! He must have been starving."

"He told the people who freed him that the roof tasted quite good."

I shook my head in wonderment.

The gypsy village resembled some of the poorest places I had seen on earth. One room homes made out of hardened mud, tacked together with discarded pieces of metal, wood, plastic, and cardboard would shelter a family of ten or more.

There was no running water and no toilets. Cooking was either over an open fire or on a wood burning mud stove. There was no electricity. However, one of the more innovative gypsies had managed to connect a line to the nearest electric pole. This free electricity was then hooked up mud shack to mud shack until the whole village was connected.

The church was a one room hovel made from mud. There was a small playground to the left of it. The building was surprisingly clean inside. Service had already begun as we walked in. The gypsies must have never seen an Asian looking face before. Their eyes bugged out of their heads as they stared at me in fascination. Everything came to a stop. A boy jostled his neighbor and shouted, "Bruce Lee!"

"Shut up, you stupid!" the neighbor shot back. "Bruce Lee is dead. It's Jackie Chan."

It reminded me of Perescu's sister, and the moon-shining mother, who had been the first to call me Jackie Chan. It crossed my mind that maybe all Asians do look like Jackie!

The news spread like wildfire that Jackie Chan had landed in the village and was preaching that morning. In a short time, the one room church was filled to the roof. Another hundred gypsies craned their necks to peek in through the sole door and window. I tried my best to explain to them that there were many Asians in this world and there was only one Jackie Chan, but to no avail.

"Jackie! Jackie!" they chanted, smiling and laughing with freedom. After I finished preaching, the chant had changed to "Jesus! Jesus!"

I couldn't help liking this humble church constructed from mud better than the whitewashed legalistic churches I had been to before.

56. Beggars or Believers?

On the drive back to the city, Credinescu and I discussed charity for and to the gypsies.

"Let me tell you something which you don't seem to be able to see," Credinescu stated.

"What do you mean?" I asked defensively.

"Do you see that gypsy over there picking through the garbage heap?"

"Yes, of course I do! I noticed for some time that only gypsies scrounge through garbage."

"Well, this came from all the 'well-meaning' foreign Christians who swamped our country after 1989 and the fall of Communism, distributing aid to the gypsies. The gypsies now expect continuous aid and will not work at all. They would rather become beggars and scavengers. There are jobs available but they refuse to work. They expect free handouts from foreigners, and have become conditioned to that way of thinking. They became beggars because of people like you!"

"Wait a second," I objected. "You cannot blame that on foreign aid. From what I heard, some gypsies did not want to work before Communism fell. So why would they want to work post-Communism?"

"Because there were no jobs for them then. Now there are but they would rather get aid instead."

"Well, I did not bring any social aid here. I came only with spiritual food."

"I did not mean you, particularly. I mean you, in a general way."

"I see what you are getting at though. Giving them aid for long periods of time without requiring them to earn it, or become responsible, actually makes them acquire a beggars' mentality. They should be believers not beggars."

"You got it!" Credinescu confirmed.

"We actually have the same problem back in America. There are generations of people who get caught up in the welfare system and now cannot get out of it."

"Same here! All these gypsies should go to work."

"I agree with you but it may not be so simple. Have you ever thought that they might need a helping hand to join society again? Also, some of them may be physically incapable of work."

"Not the gypsies. They are strong but lazy. It's the same all over Europe. The gypsies beg while the rest of the population work. Other nations accuse us of discriminating against the gypsies but we actually provide equal opportunities for them. It's just that they do not want these opportunities."

I sat back in silence and thought about Credinescu's viewpoint.

57. Corrupt Teachers

It was early one Sunday morning, before the church program began, when a couple accosted me.

"We would like you to marry us," the boy whom I did not know said.

I opened my eyes wide in surprise.

"Yes, we would like you to marry us," the girl whom I did not know, who was clinging to the arm of the boy whom I did not know, chimed in. She smiled sweetly at me.

"Who are you and why do you want me to marry you?" I asked.

The girl looked at the boy apprehensively before replying. "We are from another church and our pastor caught us holding hands."

I raised my eyebrows.

"So?"

The boy sucked in his breath and replied bravely. "Well that is a sin and we were told to leave the church. After we left, we were told by others that we had to get married because we had held hands. We couldn't go back to our church so here we are. Can you marry us?"

"Your pastor told you it's a sin to hold hands?" I asked. "And now you must get married but not at your church?"

I must have looked dumber than a squid for the couple stared back at me strangely.

"Yes! We just told you that!"

"I'm not sure what church you came from but I don't marry couples for holding hands. If you are living in sin and want to change, then yes. But you still have to go through a few months of pre-marital counseling."

It was their turn to look dumb as squids.

"You mean we don't have to get married if we hold hands?" they asked wide-eyed.

I was wondering whether I was still on Earth.

"No, you don't!" I replied emphatically. "Actually, you should get to know each other as well as possible before you get married. At your age, I suggest waiting a few years. People rush into marriage and then rush out of marriage even faster."

They smiled in relief. "What time does your program start? We would like to come to your church."

"We start at ten."

As the couple found seats at the back, I caught sight of Daliascu and beckoned to her.

"Let me pray for your upcoming exams," I said.

"I don't need prayers for my exams!" Daliascu replied.

"Don't you believe God can help you with your exams?" I asked. "God can help us in every aspect of our lives."

"Of course I do!" Daliascu said in a shocked tone. "I wasn't referring to God at all. You have been here in this country for some time now but you still do not get it."

"Get what?"

"Going to school is useless in this country!"

"I disagree. Education is very important. I should know – I have been in education almost all of my life! Why do you say that education is useless?"

The look Daliascu gave me made me feel dumber than a dead extinct dodo. Coupled with the earlier dumb squid look, I must have looked pretty dumb.

"Because in this country, there is a certain protocol!" Daliascu explained.

"What protocol?" I asked, clueless.

"Going to school is useless because if you want to pass the exams, the protocol is to pay the professors to give you a good grade. It doesn't matter how smart you are, but how much you pay!"

"I don't believe that!" I shot back. "That's just an excuse for poor performance!"

"Well then, how do you account for the fact that I have friends who do not attend classes at all, who do not even show up for exams, but they still pass with flying colors?"

I began to get interested in this alternative education system. "How much do they have to pay?"

"Anywhere from a few hundred dollars upwards."

"But doesn't the Dean or the school director do anything about this?"

"Oh, they take the biggest cut! How else do they build their mansions with their pitiful salaries?"

"But I am sure that not every student has a few hundred dollars to bribe the professors or the dean."

"Of course not! Where there's no money, there's always sex."

"Sex?"

"Yes, there are many cases of students sleeping with their professor. That helps you through all sorts of mental deficiencies. It is a common practice here. Of course, that is only viable if the professor is male. There are no lesbians here in this country."

"So money and sex gets you through school here?"

"That is the protocol. But there are other methods as well."

"Other methods?" I echoed.

"Yes, if all else fails, you can always buy forged degrees and certificates. In this country, you can buy forged high school and university diplomas, driving licenses, passports, ID cards, ATM cards, and even forged death certificates."

I was stunned. "But what use is a bought medical degree if one does not even know the basics of biology or bio-chemistry? How is the degree going to help if one does not know anything in that area?"

"It doesn't. But it will get you respect. How do you think Elena Ceausescu, wife of Nicolae Ceausescu, obtained all her chemistry degrees when she only had a fourth grade education? She didn't even know how to pronounce basic chemical compound names. Yet, she produced brilliant articles, lauded worldwide, on polymer chemistry. As I said before, you can always buy degrees and diplomas here."

"This sounds crazy!" I said.

"But a false degree will only take you so far," Daliascu continued. "You need connections too."

"Connections?"

"Because in the end, it all depends upon who you know. You can be dumber than a potato and still become a manager or a senator simply because of your family's connections. If you are commoner and do not know anybody influential, you are condemned even before you begin. That is why so many Romanians, especially the smart ones, left this country. Here, merit doesn't count: only connections and money to bribe those who have connections!"

"We can still pray for your upcoming exams," I said.

"Yes, let's," Daliascu replied. "God is all I have."

＾＊－＊の

58. Traveling First Class

"That was an interesting morning," I muttered.

Credinescu, who was helping me carry the church equipment back to my place, nodded emphatically.

"Yes, it is very interesting to serve God in this country. It gets one into all sorts of predicaments and problems."

"But none that we cannot overcome as God is on our side," I replied confidently.

"It gets tiring though."

"Yes, it does wear us down. But the main thing is to carry on and not look back. Why, what's wrong?"

Credinescu was the first to notice it.

"Your front door is missing!" Credinescu exclaimed.

I was taken aback. "What are you talking about?"

He pointed to a blank space where my front door should have been. I almost stopped breathing. The door of my apartment was missing!

"Maybe Black Bear, my landlord, is repairing something," I reasoned. "I can't think of any other explanation."

As we lugged the sound equipment into the flat, we saw the truth. Or rather we did not see it.

We did not see it because there was nothing to be seen. Some unknown person or persons had busted into the place while we were having church and cleaned it out! There was nothing left except the two ugly green chairs. All my laptops, electronics, watches, keys, appliances – everything was gone. The thieves had even stolen my travel bags to neatly pack the stolen items in. Clever of them – it was much easier and less conspicuous to haul out of the apartment travel bags, rather than armfuls of electronics and other valuables. If we hadn't been at church, all the music equipment that I had replaced would be gone too!

"Let's call the police!" Credinescu said.

"Please, do it for me," I replied, gritting my teeth. "Let me look around."

Credinescu called the police while I looked for my documents. I had stored all of my important documents between my clothes. But the robbers had gone through each and every pocket. My passport, ID cards, birth certificate, bank cards – everything was gone! It was then that I realized that my extra set of car keys were gone too. Anyone possessing those keys could drive my car away to the nearest chop shop. I sighed deeply as I waited for the police.

In the next few hours, the police came, powdered everything yellow, found nothing, blamed the gypsies, and left. I knew it could not have been the gypsies; no vagabond gypsy could have known the value of some of the missing items.

"You can sleep at my place tonight," Credinescu offered. "It may be safer for you."

"Thanks, but I'll be fine here," I replied. "I don't think they'll be back tonight. There's nothing left to steal except my car. They have my duplicate keys. Come to think of it, I might even catch the thieves if they come back for the car. The police told me to call them if I were to see anything suspicious."

"The police wouldn't come," Credinescu replied confidently. "You will have to catch the thief yourself. Are you sure you can manage that?"

"I'll call you if I need help. Then you can rush over."

"Sure thing." But his eyes belied his enthusiasm.

As night came, I propped up the busted front door over the wide open entrance with one of the green chairs. The other, I dragged next to the window, overlooking the car, and prepared to wait for the thief. But nothing happened. Nobody used the car keys that were stolen.

I tried, unsuccessfully, to catch the thief for the next three nights, before coming to the conclusion that the thieves were too busy celebrating to contend with their insomniac and paranoid victim. In the meantime, I ordered a new door. The old wooden door, supported by the two ugly chairs, made a fine table.

....

"I'm in real trouble," I confessed. "I am here in Romania and I have no identification papers whatsoever. The thieves took it all. Immigration would fine me thousands of dollars."

"The police can arrest you as an illegal and throw you in jail," Credinescu confided. "Even with papers they can still lock you up. What more without papers!"

"I'm going to the American Embassy today. They should be able to help me there."

"Why didn't you go there sooner?"

"I was busy trying to catch the thieves," I argued lamely. "But they never showed up. Thieves never show up when you want them to."

"They already cleaned you out," Credinescu pointed out. "Why would they want to come back?"

"As I told you before, I wanted to see whether they would also try to steal my car. But since I have already replaced all the locks on my car, there is no longer any sense in waiting around here."

"How much did the thieves steal?"

"Thousands! Just to replace all those stolen papers will take another ten thousand dollars minimum. I will leave for the Embassy tonight by train."

"That's a ton of losses," Credinescu replied with feeling. "I wouldn't blame you if you leave and never come back. You have gone through some pretty incredible things."

"I'm not going anywhere! As soon as I replace my papers and passport, I'll be back. Will you come and see me off at the train station?"

"Sure! That's no problem at all."

"Good! Let's meet at seven tonight at the station."

"Seven it is then."

. . . .

The train station was a monumental building matched only by its monumental disintegration. The once beautifully sculptured overhangs, now crumbling and falling, threatened pedestrians with death by concussion. The pedestrians, faces masked by concern, scooted hurriedly underneath the structure like frightened penguins jostling their way towards the ocean chased by a ravenous polar bear. Grey walls, coated with soot and dirt, and century old windows glued shut by endless coats of indistinct paint, added to this picture of decay. Mixed with the decay were hordes of beggars and gypsies, all intent on depriving the unwary and tired traveler of his or her luggage. Only a second of distraction to pay the taxi driver, a quick visit to the bathroom, or a momentary conversation with a stranger would result in the inevitable loss of one or more bags. The police were conspicuous by their absence.

I clung onto my little travel bag like a drowning, desperate man clinging onto a 5'5" blonde life preserver floating by.

"Get into the station quick!" Credinescu snapped at me. "The longer you stand out here the more of a target you become."

I needed little urging. My past experiences with street gypsies had been highly embarrassing, if not downright entertaining. We found the ticket counter.

"Would you like a first class ticket or a second class ticket?" Credinescu asked.

"What's the price difference?" I asked. "I feel very poor at present."

"Not much difference at all. You had better get a fist class ticket. People in second class sometimes drag their chickens and goats with them. You may not like to be squeezed between a couple of goats, a few hens, and some drunken peasants."

"Squeezed by goats, well, I don't think I want to be."

"There's a train at eleven and another at five tomorrow morning."

"Get me a first class ticket for the eleven o'clock train."

After I obtained my ticket, we set off to find the train. A bitingly cold wind howled miserably through the long tunnels and passages of the station. It howled like a banshee and I was reminded of an old movie, Dr. Zhivago, where the same cold aggressive wind buffeted and beat the protagonists into submission from the start to the end of the movie.

We eventually located the locomotive and the first class carriages.

"This is your carriage," Credinescu said happily.

"It cannot be," I challenged. "This carriage is sheathed in ice. It doesn't look like it has been moved since the ice age. Are you sure we have the right train?"

Credinescu looked at the ticket in my hand and reconfirmed that indeed we had located the right train.

"This is it!" he said again. "Let me help you get onboard."

We clambered with difficulty up stairs which measured four inches in width and twenty-four inches in height to be met by a disconcerting sight.

"Do you see what I am seeing?" I asked. "There's six inches of snow on the floor in this carriage. It must have blown in through the open door. I told you that this carriage looked like it had not been moved for centuries. Look at the ice on the windows! And the windows are down!"

"Stop complaining," Credinescu said. "This is first class! Think what it's like in second class!"

I hurried towards the window and tried to close it. I might as well have tried lifting the entire carriage, for it did not budge a millimeter. If this was first class, I couldn't imagine what it must have been like in second class.

We said our goodbyes and I settled down onto the tough brown leather seats - first dusting off the white carpet of snow. I was thankful to be on my way but apprehensive of the ice that coated the carriage. Yet, the ice covering the open window acted as a shield, effectively blocking the howling wind from entering the compartment. I clutched my bag tightly, waiting for the train to depart.

With surprising promptness and a mighty lurch, the carriage jolted into motion at the stroke of eleven. Unfortunately, the jolt broke the ice around the window and the wind began to howl in.

Very soon, as the train gathered speed, a snowstorm developed in my compartment. The fresh snow billowing in through the window churned the snow already on the leather seats, which whipped at the snow on the floor turning the whole place into a Christmas globe shaken by a mad man. In that wintry mess, Credinescu's words came back crustily – "Don't complain. This is first class!"

I did not complain for the first two hours. After that, as my eyeballs froze in my sockets, I started to complain. To keep myself from turning into an ice block, I started wandering the desolate hallways of the first class carriage, peeking into empty compartments, and flapping my arms vigorously. I began to doubt whether first class was really better. Maybe there was a reason why there was not a soul, bar myself, in first class. Second class would be packed with people and animals and people and animals meant warmth! I started dreaming of being trapped between warm goats.

Then as the third hour approached, I began to feel a slight inkling of approaching heat. It started as a warm glow under the brown leather seat. It spread quickly. The snow began to melt forming rivulets on the floor. The heat kept getting hotter. Very soon a fine steam enveloped the floor of the compartment. The brown leather seats started smoking! I was enjoying the heat, unconcerned, until I felt my bottom burning. Only then did I start to look around for a valve to regulate the heat. I did not find any until I overturned the seats to discover enormous boiling pipes underneath. The pipes must have been connected to the boilers in the locomotive for they were red hot. I noticed a small valve to one side of the pipes. Grasping it, I tried to twist it with all my might before I noticed that it was welded.

By this time my clothes were dripping wet from a mixture of steam and sweat. I found myself in a very strange predicament. From the floor of the train up to the window, it was a veritable sauna. Steam swirled while red hot pipes boiled merrily. Above the window that was stuck, snow billowed in with a mighty rush. This resulted in half the compartment freezing and the other half boiling! The ceiling of the train alternately froze or dripped hot water. It was like heaven and hell all mixed up. I didn't know whether to take off or put on more clothes. Confronted with this dilemma, I spent the entire journey alternating between standing on the leather seats, to cool down, and squatting on the floor, to get warmed up.

After another few hours, the train finally reached its destination.

....

Stumbling out of the train station, I was immediately met with pelting dirt. I whirled around, bag clutched around my middle like a shield, ready for an impending attack. But there was nobody near me. The only thing I saw was a lone truck making its way slowly down the icy street.

As I watched the truck's tail lights recede down the street, two apparitions, swathed completely in multiple layers of what looked like bandages, stood up at the back. Then with almost mummy like movements, the apparitions dug into the back of the truck, and heaved onto the street shovelfuls of dirt and small pebbles. As their faces were completely masked against the cold, their payloads were distributed equally between road, parked cars, and pedestrians. Two mummies flinging dirt from the back of a truck to de-ice the roads! I had never seen that back in the States.

I managed to catch the bus to the Embassy before my ears fell off in the rock-splitting cold. Even in that unearthly cold morning the bus was packed. I found myself squeezed between an old woman and a man who had his eyes tightly shut. I absorbed their warmth as I stared out of the foggy bus windows. The journey was uneventful until the bus descended an incline.

One moment the gears were screaming, the next there was absolute silence as the driver shut off the engine and allowed gravity and ice to carry the bus down the long slope. While I was familiar with the common practice of drivers switching off their car engines to conserve gas, I had never seen a bus driver doing it. The bus careened down the icy slope like a giant over stuffed coffin.

Suddenly, out of a side street, five boys on sleds shot out directly in front of the bus! Their mirth transformed into terror as they saw the bus barreling towards them - threatening to turn them into morning pancakes.

The bus driver cursed silently as he swerved madly to avoid the boys. This unexpected stratagem caused the passengers to be thrown violently: first to the left, then to the right. Shouts ensued, followed by windows being thrown down. Concerned heads popped out to inspect the carnage. Thankfully, the boys skillfully maneuvered their sleds out of harm's way and flew to either side of the bus. Seeing no carnage except the gleeful faces of the boys sledding shotgun beside the bus, concern turned to cursing instead.

However, my eyes were focused elsewhere.

During the moment of near disaster, a young man a few feet away from me had drawn out a knife! It was not as long as the knife One-Eye had used on the pig but it glinted nastily. While everybody's eyes were on what was taking place outside the bus, he quickly slit the bottom of the purse of a woman directly in front of him! The contents of the purse emptied into a prepared plastic bag which was quickly bundled up.

A few seconds later, the bus driver managed to bring his casket to a stop by slamming it into a snow bank. Everybody fell forward. The driver threw the doors open, intent on reprimanding the boys on their sleds, but was beaten out of the bus by the other young man. The young thief hopped off and quickly disappeared into the crowded morning traffic. At the same time, the woman who had been robbed started screaming!

⤙⤚

59. At the Embassy

Still reeling from the journey and the events on the bus, I reached the American Embassy. It was off the main street tucked behind an enormous hotel. My first thought upon reaching the Embassy was I had the wrong building, as it was flat and unassuming. But what stood out were the six uniformed guards outside displaying menacing machine guns; and the concrete barriers placed in front of the Embassy - effectively blocking off traffic to the entire street. The entrance was not unlike a maximum security prison. Walled with steel bars, a thick revolving turnstile gate, and miles of barbed wires, it would have fazed the most crazed zealot attempting a suicide mission.

I walked toward the steel bars.

"Stop!" a stentorian voiced barked at me. Six guns swung lazily in my direction.

"I'm just here to replace my documents which were stolen," I said, smiling pleasantly to disarm their suspicions.

"Do you have an appointment?" one of the guards asked. He was built like a tree trunk but I suspected much tougher.

"Yes, I called beforehand. The person I spoke to asked me to come in."

"Show me some identification then."

"I can't show you anything. I've been robbed and the thieves stole all my documents."

"You must have some type of ID."

"All my papers, including my passport, were stolen," I repeated.

"Show me your birth certificate then."

"That was stolen too."

"Driving license?"

"Stolen."

"What do you have?"

"Nothing!" I replied.

"Then you stay outside!" the guard said in defiance. He fingered his machine gun, showing me that he meant business.

"I tell you that I'm from America."

"No, you're not. Americans are white and you are not."

"Not all Americans are white," I explained patiently.

He eyed me suspiciously. "You don't have a passport and you don't look like an American. And you want to enter the embassy?"

"Yes," I replied. "Look, what am I supposed to do now? I traveled all night to be here."

"I don't know and I don't care," the guard said. "Now, please, move back ten meters from the embassy or we will move you back!" The other five guards, all resembling tree trunks, glared down at me.

At that moment, an employee of the embassy walked out. As she walked past, I pounced on her. I explained my situation to her amidst the disapproving glares of the guards.

"When I get back, I will check our database in Vienna," she replied. "If you can provide all the required information, we will help you get back to the States - although, it may take a while."

"Thank-you!"

True to her word, I was led into the embassy after a few hours wait. While some other personnel were verifying the database in Vienna, Austria, I struck up a conversation with the staff member who had let me in. I explained my situation to her.

"The police told me that the culprits were gypsies but I am not so sure."

"That is not a new story," she replied. "These things do happen quite often in Romania. I have a personal friend at another embassy who told me his story. He was to be the new chargé d'affaires in Romania, temporarily replacing the outgoing ambassador. It was his first trip to Eastern Europe and he was naturally curious about the place. After his plane landed, instead of heading directly to his embassy, he caught a taxi to the city center. As he got out of the taxi, a group of gypsies attacked him and stole all his luggage, money and other personal belongings. He did not speak Romanian, so nobody could understand his pleas for help. He ended up spending his first day, as an official diplomat, in the city jail."

"What happened to him then?"

"He asked to be sent home immediately after getting out of prison!"

I made sympathetic noises.

"That's not so bad," she continued. 'One German businessman lost his way driving through the mountains and somehow, got himself stranded without gas in a remote village. He not only lost all his valuables but his life as well. Some shepherds found his mutilated body in a nearby field some days later. The police believe that the gypsies living in the village committed the crime."

"Wow!" I exclaimed. "I'm glad I just lost my documents."

After my papers were sorted out at the Embassy, I hastily made my way back to the train station. Arriving at the ticket counter, a portly woman with fire engine red hair barked at me. "Do you want a first class or second class ticket?"

I did not hesitate this time. "I'll take second class please! I like goats!"

Thankfully she did not call me a billy-goat as she handed the ticket over.

When I reached back home, I found an anonymous letter in my mailbox. It informed me that Mrs. Urdescu, the Communist spy living in the apartment beneath mine, had orchestrated the break-in into my apartment. The letter further informed me that that was payback for the water damage to her apartment from my bathroom incident. The letter also implicated Mrs. Urdescu in the car spotting incident. I stared at the letter for a long time as some of these incidents had occurred a long time ago. If true, I guess spies, like elephants, never forget. On the other hand, since everybody in the block hated Mrs. Urdescu, I wondered about the veracity of the letter. I decided, true or not, to forgive her too.

It took almost two weeks before I obtained a new credit card. With the new card, I managed to book my plane tickets back to New York. When I received my new passport, I flew back to Romania to continue with the church.

60. The Hit Man and Conversations with God IV

Walking into church, I saw Daliascu. She was motioning me to come over. She seemed agitated and nervous. I walked over expecting a warm Welcome Back reception.

"My father has hired a hit-man to get you!" Daliascu said, bluntly.

"Say that again."

"Just what I said: He has hired a hit-man to get rid of you."

"Why do people here want to kill missionaries?" I asked.

"He doesn't want to kill missionaries; he just wants to kill you."

"But why?"

"Well, because I became a Christian and got baptized!"

"That's not a good enough reason to have me bumped off!"

"It is to him. My becoming a Christian is like losing a daughter. He will become a laughing-stock to his friends and to our family. It does not matter to him if I do drugs or end up in prison as long as I do not convert and become a Christian. This is the biggest insult possible!"

"I wonder if other parents want me dead too?"

"They probably do!" Daliascu confirmed. "I suggest you stay indoors or go back home."

"Well, I just got back and I have to go out and meet people. I cannot stay indoors out of fear."

"The hit-man can get you anytime, anywhere! The hit-man may show up here, at the school gym, while we are having church and kill you in front of everyone."

"I will just have to take my chances. For now, let us pray for him."

"Pray for the hit-man? Are you crazy?"

"No! I mean let's pray for your father. God may soften his heart to the point where he cancels the hit."

"That will be long after you are dead!"

I stared at her and wondered how long I had to live.

. . . .

After church, I went back into my prayer closet to talk to my Father.

"Things have gotten worse, Father. Last time, I lost a car then I lost everything in the break-in. But now I may lose my life. I want to be focused on ministry but it's hard when a hit man is after me. I remember that you taught me the difference between 'interested' and 'committed' people. I am staying committed to Your calling, but I do not know how long I can stay committed."

God showed me something brand new that day. "Your position is not unique. Many missionaries are called to move beyond the words in My book to a heightened spiritual reality, where by personal experience, My words become alive. You will not just read about the truth, but be *in* the truth. You will see, hear, feel, smell, and taste My truth. You will love those who despitefully use you and you will share My unconditional love to those who persecute you. Can you love My people at this level? For commitment is only for a period of time. But I am seeking people who will serve me for a lifetime. I am looking for loyal people. Can you be loyal to Me?"

I didn't know what to answer. I felt so inadequate. "I will try," I whispered.

My mind went back to the day when I had first landed in Romania. Flashbacks of gypsies, dogs, sausages, spies, tricksters, lawyers, guns, orphans, religious and legalistic people, immigration officers, lard, coffins, disappearing cars, and thieves swirled in my mind. Would I be able to survive more challenges to become a loyal servant? More importantly, would the people in my church survive the beatings and persecutions?

Would I survive the hit placed on me?

The great adventure with God had begun.

ॐॐ

61. Epilogue

Romania ascended to North Atlantic Treaty Organization (NATO) in 2004 and to the European Union (EU) in 2007. Much has changed since then.

After British Broadcasting Corporation (BBC) reporters infiltrated the worst state orphanages, much in the same way I did, and reported on the appalling conditions there, the hell-house orphanages have closed and the unwanted children placed in foster care. The still functioning orphanages are now better managed and the suffering of the orphans alleviated or at least, ameliorated. In the last few years, I had the pleasure of visiting many very well run orphanages, both state and private. Unfortunately, cases of children being chained and tied up are still practiced in remote villages.

The government has attempted to integrate gypsies into the society, but so far, with minimum success. The gypsies continue to feel discriminated against and consequently, have moved en masse out of Romania to neighboring European countries. In Italy, entire gypsy shanty towns have sprung up overnight around Rome and other major cities. These have caused the Italian police massive headaches in terms of rising crime. The Italians have even resorted to the local mafia for help in curtailing this tide of new immigrants. The mafia's solution was to torch the shantytowns. However, the gypsies have not helped their plight by engaging in criminal acts ranging from murders, rapes, to the kidnapping of Italian babies.

In Austria, the gypsies had to take flight after eating all the swans in the manicured lakes and gardens of 'The Sound of Music' fame. Now swan-less, the Austrians were also clueless on how to get the gypsies out of Austria. Neighboring France thought of a solution – direct cash payments for gypsies who choose to go back to Romania to begin micro-farms. One indelible picture is forever etched in my mind – that of a gypsy woman laughing out loud, with pronounced gold teeth, clutching 3,000 Euros (US$4500) in her hand, boarding a free flight home, and shouting at the top of her voice, "Long live France! You stupid people, I will be back here in two weeks! I don't even know what a micro-farm is! Thanks for the money though."

Corruption is rampant in Romania. The government has attempted to clean up this area but in vain. Nearly every aspect of Romanian life is permeated with corruption. In a recent swoop by the new National Anti-Corruption Directorate (DNA), many government employees were arrested for selling fake drivers' licenses, identification cards, and school diplomas. But when corruption is at the top, it follows that the whole body is corrupt. At the top, judges and politicians are bribed by people to look favorably their way. At the bottom, bus and train conductors are bribed by passengers to look the other way while they travel ticketless. At the side, football players and referees are bribed by competing clubs to throw matches.

In 2008, Robert De Niro, the famous actor was arrested in a roadside check in Romania. Upon closer examination, the police concluded that the driver was in fact not the real De

Niro but an imposter with impeccably forged papers. I am still waiting for the police to catch the US president or the Pope, speeding recklessly through a remote mountain village somewhere in the Carpathian Mountains.

In another case, a bank manager managed to obtain all of his employees' identification cards, secured huge loans in their favor, then transferred all the monies into his personal account before absconding with the loot. The employees only became aware of their boss's deception after receiving a letter from the bank asking them to pay back the multi million-dollar loan so fortuitously granted to them one month earlier.

While there are many people in the country who try to be honest and abide by the law, they find themselves obliged to work with corruption or not work at all. In a deeply flawed system, corruption flourishes. A prime example of this is in the medical profession. Young doctors, who in principle may be against bribery, are chastised and threatened with dismissal by established doctors if they do not tow the line and accept bribes from their patients. A younger doctor who exhibits an inordinate amount of concern and care for his or her patients may also be reprimanded. This is because the practice of such 'free' care for patients may dent the bribes necessary for sustaining such care.

When asked about such practices, an older doctor confided to me, "The patients themselves expect to pay us bribes! If we don't take the bribes proffered, they take it as a sign that their disease is incurable and therefore hopeless. Therefore, we have to take bribes to give hope to our patients and allay their anxiety. Taking bribes helps our patients stay alive!"

In the education front, due to the corruption among teachers, the smart and young have abandoned their trust in formal education and are instead, utilizing their considerable talents in the art of phishing, ATM fraud, and terrorizing American eBay users.

Despite the widespread corruption, slowly, but surely, a small but well educated, middle-class is forming in the country. Unfortunately but true, in 2009, Berlin-based nongovernmental organization, Transparency International, rated Romania as the most corrupt EU nation.

Since EU accession, Romania has been given billions of Euros for infrastructure repair and development. This has helped upgrade and repair the broken roads and highways in the country. Unfortunately, corners were cut and monies siphoned off. Roads, only one year old, literally disintegrated and had to be torn up and replaced. A report in 2008 put Romania as only ten years behind other Eastern European countries in this area. Still the country is enjoying an unprecedented economic boom with an annual growth rate of approximately 7-8%. Sustaining this growth has become a top priority for the government.

In a similar vein, billions of Euros earmarked for farm improvement, were mismanaged as well. Funds meant for farm improvement funneled into the pockets of the administrators instead of the farmers. This led to a suspension of sorely needed future farm aid from the EU.

When the government started de-classifying and releasing Communist era secret files, it was discovered that the files juxtaposed measured eight miles in length. Eight miles of wiretapping, surveillance, and reports on its own citizens! Like farm aid, I believe that with careful management, all the files could have fitted on one external hard drive, measuring less than a foot.

Butchering pigs and spies in front of apartment blocks is now illegal. New European laws require humane killing methods. However, most Romanians still prefer the nine-inch knife to solve their problems.

The stray dogs continue to be sterilized and they continue to multiply. This perversion of biological laws has left many city administrations scratching their heads in bafflement. When President Bush visited Romania in 2008, the security detail closed off all the roads and sealed all the sewer holes that the Presidential motorcade would traverse through. The sewer children did not pop up, but nobody informed the dogs and they popped up unexpectedly, stopping an entire Presidential motorcade by their brazen wanderings.

Credit started in earnest after 2007. Now free from the constraints of using only cash, many Romanians have joined their Western counterparts in buying things they do not need at prices they cannot afford. The country continues to be a very rich country full of very poor people.

Paradoxically, the latest unofficial EU survey found the Romanian market most lucrative for luxury items. The newly rich easily beat out the rest of Europe for high-end goods consumption, like Ferraris, Lamborghinis, and yachts. It can be safely concluded that in Romania, Lamborghinis now share the highways with horse drawn carts hewn from trees. The horses do much better on certain parts of the highway due to their innate ability to traverse through craters.

There are about 3 to 4 million Romanians working legally and illegally outside the country. This is roughly 15-20% of the total population. The reason for this mass exodus of the labor force is that while prices of food and other products have risen 10-15 times in the last few years, salaries have remained low. As salaries are much higher in other EU countries, Romanians have been forced to work outside the country to make a decent living. However, this phenomenon has exacerbated the problem of children being left alone while both parents work outside the country. But as salaries continue to grow in the country, some of those who left may be tempted to move back.

Romanians, in general, are very warm, friendly, and giving people. However, they tend to view foreigners with suspicion. But when a foreigner is accepted as part of their family, they will protect and defend that person with their lives. Now, with the possibility of worldwide travel without restrictions, many Romanians are beginning to lose their suspicious nature.

After EU ascension, the spiritual climate of the country has moved dramatically towards indifference. The majority of the population sees God as irrelevant in their daily lives. Those who seek out God continue to be abused by extreme religion, control, and legalism. A law was recently passed which prohibits the setup of a new church unless the church can prove it has 23,000 members. As most new churches struggle with congregations ranging from twenty to fifty, this new law effectively shelters the existing churches from any serious revival. It is almost miraculous how in a country with so many church buildings, there can be so little God.

Modern worship is now part of the youth-church culture. I am honored to have played a part in making this happen. I brought modern worship to Romania more than a decade ago. In this time, youth from other churches had visited my church, learned the songs, and taken them back to their respective youth groups. In turn, they had faced condemnation and persecution for worshipping with modern 'satanic' instruments like the drums. Nevertheless, modern worship is now flourishing all over the country.

Despite all these obstacles, the good news of Jesus Christ is being shared and people continue to be set free as God's plan for Romania marches on.

Additional copies of this book can be obtained through the author's website at *www.witnessingtodracula.com* or at *www.amazon.com*

To share your comments, personal mission stories, or read what other people are saying about this book, go to *Facebook* and become a fan of *Witnessingtodracula* homepage.